本成果受到浙江海洋大学外国语学院学科建设经费资助,在此致谢。

托妮·莫里森的儒家思想研究

Reading Toni Morrison's Novels in the Viewpoint of Confucianism

张贝　著

浙江工商大学出版社
ZHEJIANG GONGSHANG UNIVERSITY PRESS
·杭州·

图书在版编目(CIP)数据

托妮·莫里森的儒家思想研究 / 张贝著. —杭州：
浙江工商大学出版社,2022.10
ISBN 978-7-5178-5020-5

Ⅰ.①托… Ⅱ.①张… Ⅲ.①莫里森(Morrison,
Toni 1931-)—小说研究②儒家—哲学思想—研究 Ⅳ.
①I712.074②B222.05

中国版本图书馆 CIP 数据核字(2022)第114062号

托妮·莫里森的儒家思想研究
TUONI MOLISEN DE RUJIA SIXIANG YANJIU

张贝　著

责任编辑	张莉娅	
责任校对	鲁燕青	
封面设计	浙信文化	
责任印制	包建辉	
出版发行	浙江工商大学出版社	
	（杭州市教工路198号　邮政编码310012)	
	（E-mail:zjgsupress@163.com）	
	（网址:http://www.zjgsupress.com）	
	电话:0571-88904980,88831806(传真)	
排　　版	杭州朝曦图文设计有限公司	
印　　刷	杭州宏雅印刷有限公司	
开　　本	710mm×1000mm　1/16	
印　　张	13.25	
字　　数	216千	
版 印 次	2022年10月第1版　2022年10月第1次印刷	
书　　号	ISBN 978-7-5178-5020-5	
定　　价	68.00元	

Confucian Terms Used in This Book

Below is a list of key Chinese terms with variants of their translation. It is important to note that sometimes, instead of the Chinese terms, a variant of its translation appears in the entry.

chi 耻 shameful

dao 道 Way

de 德 virtue

e 恶 vile, morally culpable

he 和 harmony

he er butong 和而不同 harmony but not uniformity

jianai 兼爱 universal love and mutual benefit

junzi 君子 a gentleman, great man, an exemplary man

li 利 profit

li 理 order, law, principle

li 礼 rites, ritual propriety, social norms

meng yi yangzheng 蒙以养正 enlightening the ignorant and making them follow the right path

ming 命 destiny

qizhi zhi xing 气质之性 character endowed by *qi*

tianming zhi xing 天命之性 character endowed by Heaven

ren 仁 humane, humaneness

ru 儒 ritual specialists and professional men with textual knowledge

shan 善 goodness

sheng 圣 sage

shu 恕 putting oneself in the other person's place

tian 天 Heaven

tianming 天命 what Heaven decreed, what Heaven intended

tianren ganying 天人感应 human and Heaven respond to each other

tianren xiangfen 天人相分 distinction between human and Heaven

wen 文 culture, cultural refinement

xiao 孝 filial piety

xiaoren 小人 a petty man

xin 信 trust, trustworthy

xing 性 human nature

xing 行 deed, conduct, action

xue 学 learning

yan 言 words, speech

yi 義 rightness, fairness

yong 勇 courage, brave

zheng 政 to govern, to rule, government

zheng 正 to correct, to rectify, upright

zhengming 正名 rectifying names

zhi 知 to know, to understand

zhi 直 upright, uprightness

zhong 忠 to do the best, be loyalty

Foreword

    This book aims to study Toni Morrison's works in the viewpoint of Confucianism, which is the core of Chinese traditional philosophy. It focuses on the relationship between Heaven and human, aiming to reach the harmony and coexistence of Heaven and human. The reason for doing this research derives from Morrison's connection with Confucianism. Morrison has been to China and experienced Chinese life based on Confucianism in the 1980s. Maxine Hong Kingston, who is a Chinese American female writer, has been a literary friend with Morrison for a long time. It is natural that they have influenced each other on their thoughts. Morrison's experience as an editor in Random House led her to learn the Eastern philosophy. There are some books about Confucius and Confucianism that have been published in Random House. In addition, a lot of critics have proved that Morrison's writing and thought has been influenced by Ralph Waldo Emerson and Henry David Thoreau's philosophy which is related to Confucianism. Ralph Waldo Emerson and Henry David Thoreau are American philosophers who are interested in Confucianism and influenced by Confucius greatly. It is certain that Morrison learned Confucianism or that she got influenced by Confucianism through the two famous transcendentalists Emerson and Thoreau. The fact that Morrison's profound views on interrelationships, such as race relations, gender relations, familial relations, and relations between nature and human have a lot in common with Confucianism is the most convincing proof that she was influenced by Confucianism. This is why this book analyzes Morrison's novels with Confucianism. While Confucianism is a broad and systematic philosophy, this book focuses on the thought of "unity of Heaven and human" (*tianren heyi*, 天人

合一），which explores the relationship between human and nature, human and society, human and self. The author examines Morrison's novels from the three categories of relationships embedded in "unity of Heaven and human".

Toni Morrison, a famous contemporary writer, is the only African American female writer who has won the Nobel Prize in Literature. Her works describe African Americans' traumatic life and history with excellent description which shows her splendid writing skills and profound thoughts. The topics of Morrison's literary works revolve around African Americans' trauma from racial, cultural, and social perspectives. She depicts their miserable experience and analyzes the reasons of their trauma in the white-dominated society. Through depicting the life and destiny of various characters in her works, Morrison illustrates the necessity of human beings to keep a healthy and harmonious relationship with nature, with other people, and with the inner self to become authentic human beings. As a humanistic writer, Morrison is also concerned about the destiny and development of the whole human beings. She endeavors to explore the effective ways to achieve the harmonious relationship between human, nature, society, and self. Confucian "unity of Heaven and human" also explores the relationship between Heaven and human. The main ideas of this thought revolve around the relationship between human and nature, human and society, and human with the self.

Confucian "unity of Heaven and human" holds that human and nature are interdependent and inseparable in the universe. Nature not only provides material resources with which human can survive but also spiritual support for them. Human should respect and protect nature, and conform to natural laws. It advocates the mutual-respect and harmonious connection between human and nature. Among Morrison's works, there are many descriptions of human attitudes and behaviors toward nature. Some of her characters fail to realize the significant role of nature to human and destroy nature mercilessly, leading to their self-destruction. Whereas, those people who keep an intimate relationship with nature not only meet their material needs but also gain spiritual support from nature.

Through examining the harmonious and disharmonious relationships between human and nature in Morrison's novels, the thought of Confucianism is reflected vividly in her writing.

Confucian "unity of Heaven and human" also proposes to establish a harmonious relationship with family members and other people in society. It believes that family is a very important place for children's growth. The relationship between parents and children has a great influence on children's physical and mental development. Parents are the first teacher to children in their moral education and well-being. Meanwhile, children should love and respect their parents with filial piety, which is the basic characteristic of being a human. Confucianism thinks that everyone lives with various kinds of relationships in society, and deals with these social relations with humanity and morality. In Morrison's novels, the characters usually suffer some ethical crisis because of their distorted familial and social relations. The failure of constructing a harmonious relationship with other people in life leads to the incompleteness of one's self-identity. Through these characters' lives, Morrison emphasizes the importance of maintaining a healthy and harmonious relationship with other people in family and society. By exploring these relations in her works, Morrison aims to call for the elimination of different kinds of discrimination between people, and to establish harmonious social relations advocated by Confucianism. It is evident that both Confucian "unity of Heaven and human" and Morrison emphasize the importance of establishing harmonious relationships with other people in family and society.

The unity of human with his self is the highest goal pursued by Confucian "unity of Heaven and human". It believes that human beings need to keep a harmonious relationship with the inner self to construct a complete self-identity, and to attach great importance to morality and virtue and the sense of self-love and self-value in humans' self-identity construction. Through her works, Morrison describes some characters with spiritual barrenness, suffering from an internal crisis of incoherence and instability. She also depicts several characters with a harmonious spiritual world and has established a complete self-identity in life. Morrison explores ways to achieve self-affirmation and construct their identities. She points out that morality and virtues are the basic requirements for self-identity construction. Apart from morality and virtues, self-love and self-value are also indispensable to the establishment of authentic self-hood. Both "unity of Heaven and human" and Morrison emphasize the necessity of harmony between man and the inner self. The proper way to achieve this goal is to cultivate morality and virtues as well as possess the sense of self-love and self-value.

Abundant criticisms and studies have been done with Morrison's eleven novels. Because of Morrison's racial identity as an African American woman, her early writing is mainly about the racial, gender, and class discrimination of African Americans. Later Morrison expands her writing from focusing on the destiny of African Americans to the development of the whole humankind. By describing characters' harmonious and disharmonious relationships with nature, society, and self, Morrison demonstrates the importance of keeping these three relationships harmonious. These three relationships are essential in humans' self-identity construction and social development. By analyzing Morrison's works with Confucian "unity of Heaven and human", it helps us better understand Morrison's thinking and writing beneath her portrayal of the characters. This book breaks the limit of the previous studies which only interpret her novels from the racial, gender, class, and other perspectives, and expands the research scope of her novels with Confucianism.

Contents

Chapter 1 Introduction ···1

  1.1 Toni Morrison and Her Works ·······················1

  1.2 Literature Review·······································19

  1.3 Significance and Methods ···························24

  1.4 Confucian "Unity of Heaven and Human" ··············28

  1.5 Outline of the Book ·································51

Chapter 2 Relationship Between Human and Nature·············**55**

  2.1 Disharmonious Relationship Between Human and Nature ··········59

    2.1.1 Destruction and Domination of Nature ···········59

    2.1.2 Alienation from Nature·························67

  2.2 Harmonious Relationship Between Human and Nature·········75

    2.2.1 Natural Lifestyle ····························77

    2.2.2 Spiritual Support from Nature ·················85

Chapter 3 Relationship Between Human and Society·············**95**

  3.1 Relationship Between Parents and Children ·············96

    3.1.1 Distorted Paternal Love ······················97

    3.1.2 Abnormal Maternal Love ·····················105

    3.1.3 Filial Piety of Children ·······················113

  3.2 Social Relationship with Others in Society ·············119

    3.2.1 Distorted Social Relations ····················120

3.2.2 Construction of Harmonious Social Relations ·····················129

Chapter 4 Relationship Between Human and Self ·················**142**

4.1 Loss of Self-Identity Caused by Disharmonious Relationship with Self ···144

4.1.1 Lack of Morality and Virtues ······························144

4.1.2 Lack of Self-Love and Self-Value ······················153

4.2 Construction of Harmonious Relationship with Self ···············161

4.2.1 Exploration of Morality and Virtues ·················161

4.2.2 Awareness of Self-Love and Self-Value·················170

Chapter 5 Conclusion ···**176**

Bibliography ···**184**

Acknowledgement ··**196**

Chapter 1

Introduction

1.1 Toni Morrison and Her Works

Toni Morrison was born on February 18, 1931 in Lorain, Ohio, America. She was a prominent contemporary African American female writer and literary critic. Morrison was awarded the Nobel Prize in Literature in 1993, and has undoubtedly become a major voice among black writers. Her father worked in a shipyard and her mother worked as a domestic helper for the whites. Morrison grew up in a big family, in which her grandmother and mother were good at telling the black folk tale. And her grandfather and father were familiar with traditional black Blues music. They told their children stories and sang songs. After dinner, her grandmother would sometimes take out her violin and everyone would dance. And no matter how many times her mother told the ghost stories, Morrison always wanted to hear more. Her mother recalled in a 1982 interview with the *Lorain Journal*, "Finally I'd get tired of telling the stories over and over again, so I made up a new story." Her mother's stories sparked Morrison's imagination. Morrison fell in love with spoken language. All of her family members were proud of the black culture, and she learned countless black songs and stories of the black people.

In 1949, Morrison entered Howard University in Washington, D.C., one of the nation's most reputable black colleges, studying English and classic literature. After college, she continued her master study of literature at Cornell University, during which time her interest focused on William Faulkner and Virginia Woolf's novels. Her writing style was greatly influenced by the streams of consciousness skills of these two famous novelists. Afterward, she worked as a teacher at Texas Southern University, Howard University and Princeton University until retirement. During the teaching period, Morrison was concerned more about history, politics, and especially literature. Literature played an important part in the race history of America, and Morrison looked at the configuration of blackness, notions of racial purity, and how literature employed skin color to depict characters. All these contributed to the awakening of her racial consciousness. From then on, racial and cultural identity and the black culture became Morrison's lifelong consideration, and she began to use her writing to protect and promote the black culture.

Morrison's success in fiction partly relied on her experience as an editor in Random House from 1965 to 1984. She was the first African American female senior editor at Random House. During that period, she was able to get an abundant of real materials about the black people's history, which provided a lot of resources for her writing. Morrison had edited a series of books on black literature, history, and biography. For instance, in 1974, she assembled *The Black Book, Race-ing Justice, En-Gendering Power: Essays on Anita Hill, Clarence Thomas, and the Construction of Social Reality* which was called "a scrapbook of African American experience" and contains photograph, news clippings, sheet music, postcards and other ephemera. Through these materials, she gained a comprehensive and clear understanding of African Americans and a deep reflection on the issue of race. Moreover, she had edited, compiled, and published works for more than ten African American writers, such as Gayl Jones, Toni Cade Bambara, and Angela Davis, among others. She published a series of speeches on literary criticism, like *Playing in the Dark: Whiteness and the Literary Imagination* which was published in 1992. The essays in this collection explore the haunting presence of blackness within the predominately white American literary canon. Her work as an editor at Random House demonstrated a unique commitment to writers of color, and helped in opening industry doors to them.

With a profound knowledge of the black history, Morrison mainly addresses herself to examination of the history, culture, and life of African Americans. The central theme of Morrison's novels is African Americans' struggle to find self-identity and their cultural identity in an unjust society. Her novels bear witness to their physical and psychological trauma distinctively caused by the slavery system, and expose the economic, social, and cultural marginalization and oppression they are suffering. Morrison depicts African Americans' inner world with a unique and realistic viewpoint to call readers' attention to the plight of African Americans. At the same time, she is also aware of African Americans' ability to define themselves and to find their own living space within the white-dominated society.

The black community is one of Morrison's concerns in her works. Besides, Morrison considers capitalism and materialism as a corruptive and insidious perversion of human worth; she advocates the traditional African culture and values in her novels to arouse the spiritual depravity of the bourgeois' value. The main objectives of her writing are to restore the black culture, avoid alienation between the black people, and to establish the black cultural identity.

Morrison prefers to be called "a black woman novelist" rather than a "great American novelist" or a "wonderful woman novelist":

> So I've just insisted—insisted upon being called a black woman novelist. And I decided what that meant in terms of this world that has become broader and deeper through the process of reclamation because I have claimed it. I have claimed what I know. As a black and a woman, I have had access to a range of emotions and perceptions that were unavailable to people who were neither. (Taylor-Guthrie, 1994: 243)

She believes that with the identity of the black and woman, she has a deeper perception of the lives and inner world of African Americans, especially of the African American women. In the literary world, African American male writers are acquainted with a "double consciousness" for their American and black identity. As Morrison is an African American woman, she has one more consciousness than African American male: a "triple consciousness". She is always conscious of her identity as an American, an African American, and a woman. She is a carrier of plural cultural identity. As an American, Morrison has occupied an important status in the mainstream literary world of America. As an African, she has a strong sense of black race identity due to her love of the black race and culture. As an African American female, she concerns the experience and destiny of African American women in society. Female consciousness is very distinct in her works. Morrison tries hard to show the triple oppression that African American women suffered from racial and gender oppression.

Although her novels typically concentrate on African American women, Morrison refuses to identify herself as a feminist:

> To be as free as I possibly can in my imagination, I can't take positions that are closed. Everything I've ever done, in the writing world, has been to expand articulation, rather than to close it, to open doors, sometimes, not even closing the book—leaving the endings open for interpretation, re-visitation, a little ambiguity, I detest and loathe [those categories]. I think it's off-putting to some readers, who may feel that I'm involved in writing some kind of feminist tract. I don't subscribe to patriarchy, and I don't think it should be substituted with matriarchy. I think it's a question of equitable access, and opening doors to all sorts of things. (Taylor-Guthrie, 1994: 210)

Morrison has committed to the writing of the black race and the black culture. She never makes her works limited to the gender sense, but tries to make the voice of African Americans heard by the American mainstream society and promotes the culture and spirit of the black race.

As a distinctive African American female literary giant, Morrison has received a lot of honors. Such as the Anisfield-Wolf Book Award in Race

Relations, MLA Commonwealth Award in Literature, Commander of the Arts and Letters, National Humanities Medal, and so on. Those honors have established her position in the outstanding contemporary American literary world. In 1993, Morrison was awarded the Nobel Prize in Literature for she was the one "who in novels characterized by visionary force and poetic import, gives life to an essential aspect of American reality" (Taylor-Guthrie, 1994: 6). It was the first time the prize was awarded to an African American woman writer. It represented a new era of the black literature and the validity of the black woman's voice in the literary world.

Toni Morrison endeavors to make African Americans visible, their voices heard and their identities acknowledged by the white-dominated society. She demonstrates their traumas with delicate strokes, vivid characters, poetic languages, well-designed story plots, and rich imagination. Moreover, Morrison presents the unique merit and values of African Americans with various themes and stories. Criticism and reception of her novels demonstrate that her influence on the American literary world is impossible to be ignored.

Morrison is well-known for writing about her ethnic group with an intra-racial and interracial relationship in her novels. She has published a rich collection of works, including novels, essays, periodical collections, a short story, a play, etc. She mainly pays her attention to the life of African Americans and writes a series of novels, including *The Bluest Eyes* (1967), *Sula* (1973), *Song of Solomon* (1977), *Tar Baby* (1981), *Beloved* (1987), *Jazz* (1992), *Paradise* (1998), *Love* (2003), *A Mercy* (2008), *Home* (2012) and the newly published *God Help the Child* (2015). Morrison's other works including a short novel *Recitatif* (1983), a play *Dreaming Emmett* (1986), and an essay "Playing in the Dark: Whiteness and the Literary Imagination" (1992). It is composed of 25,000 copies of her collected papers.

Morrison's writing career can be roughly divided into three stages: the first stage (1970−1980) covers her first three novels, *The Bluest Eye* (1970), *Sula* (1973), and *Song of Solomon* (1980). During this period, Morrison is much concerned about the issue of race and the racial features of African American women. In these three novels, a majority of African American women are victims of the white standard of beauty. The second stage (1981–1992) of her writing includes *Tar Baby* (1981), *Beloved* (1987), *Jazz* (1992), in which Morrison, despite her concern of racism, pays more attention to the conflict between African American men and women, and between individual and community. Morrison explores the significance of acquiring self-identity and cultural identity within the collective efforts of the black people and community. When Morrison enters her third stage of writing (1993–2015), *Paradise* (1998), *Love* (2003), *A Mercy* (2008), *Home* (2012) and *God Help the Child* (2015) have been published. And she tactically focuses on the intercommunications among female characters or between opposite sexes, extending her profound concern from the black community to humankind as a whole. Different from the previous two stages, there is no specific protagonist but a collective depiction of the lives of the African American men and women.

Morrison's writing career was much influenced by the political propositions and intraracial relationship in the 1960s, when the Black Nationalist movement was flourishing. The Black Power movement, which claimed the same social, economic and political rights as the white, began after the failure of the Civil Rights movement. However, the African Americans' hope to integrate with the white society failed. This movement meant three things to African Americans, as Ronald S. Copeland states:

> What did we actually mean when we referred to the concept of Black Power? In those days it meant three things: (1) we wanted to establish an economic base within the black community. How we were to do this? Through a collective effort of black people we would pool our financial resources and purchase many of the tenements, many of the stores that existed in the black community. (2) Through collective efforts we would stop

the exploitation of our people and have the money remain in the ghetto; previously it has been taken out of it and into the suburbs. This is how we hoped to establish a black economic base. (3) Black Power also meant a new political awareness. Not just political consciousness, but electoral politics, in which we would seek out and elect those blacks who could best represent us in the state legislatures, Congress, the local councils, or other bodies. That was the political power we were talking about building in the black community. (Copeland, 1971: 235)

It is clear that African Americans hope to establish an independent community with economic basis and political rights. However, most of the white Americans regard them as a group of miserable people whose life only concerns racial issues without their own culture.

In "A Century of Negro Portraiture in American Literature" (1966), Sterling A. Brown makes a detailed study on the portrayal of African Americans in each period of America. Brown indicates that during the period of 1920s, the white writers started to address African Americans' life and characters in American literature, but their representation of the characters was conformed to racial mythes rather than real African American life and experience. In the 1930s, the white writers still failed to give African Americans an authentic literary image and stereotyped them as "self-respecting, virile, quiet but strong, slowly but surely awakened, capable of the greatest trust, willing and ready to die for the causes of race advance and economic brotherhood" (Hayden, 1996: 263). Things became better after the 1930s, when African American characters acquired a new, genuine representation in works of some white writers, such as William Faulkner.

It is during the 1960s when the Black Power movement demanded the independence of the black that Morrison began her literary career. Its political requirements and aesthetic prescriptions greatly influenced Morrison as well as other African American writers during that period. In the white writers' works, the black community was white-related and homogeneous in the white-dominated society. That meant there was not much difference among African Americans' lives since they all lived under racial oppression. Morrison contradicted this opinion by depicting a highly heterogeneous community in which everyone had a distinctive personality and life experience.

In an interview with Robert Stepto in 1991, Morrison said that she intended to make "the town, the community, the neighborhood, as strong as a character" rather than make it "The Town, they". For Morrison, the most extraordinary thing about the African Americans is that they are distinct and different from each other in behaviors and minds. Naming is the method that Morrison adopts to demonstrate various people and communities in her works. Morrison gives her characters specific names to show their identities in society. There are more than fifty people have names in *The Bluest Eye*, over thirty names have been mentioned in *Sula*, about forty names mentioned in *Song of Solomon*, over twenty in *Tar Baby*, more than ten in *Beloved,* and about twenty in *Jazz*. More than one hundred people have their names listed in *Paradise*, and over forty people named in *Love*, about twenty people named in *A Mercy*, over fifty names are mentioned in *Home*, and about twenty people named in Morrison's last novel, *God Help the Child*. Morrison gives these anonymous people identities by naming them and also tells the stories of them to reveal their unique life experience and distinctive personalities, which completes her aim to show the heterogeneous features of the African Americans' life and black community.

From the above examination, we can see that Morrison's community is heterogeneous rather than homogeneous. She takes great efforts to name her characters and tell their stories distinctively. To name these characters is to show respect to them and restore their humanity and identity. In this way, she not only shows the most fascinating things about the African Americans but also demolishes the white-dominated writers' thought that African Americans and community are homogenous without any distinctive features and culture. Another distinctive characteristic of Morrison's writing is that she adds so many incredible and mysterious things into her novels. For example, the dead girl spirit occurs in her fifth novel, *Beloved*, and the myth of flying in *Song of Solomon*. Morrison believes that these discredited things and black magic are part of the black culture. They are nothing but a way that black people employ to view the world, just as Morrison says:

> In addition to the very shrewd, down-to-earth, efficient way in which they did things and survived things, there was this other knowledge or perception, always discredited but there, which informed their sensibilities and clarified their activities. If formed a kind of cosmology that is perceptive as well as enchanting... (Taylor-Guthrie, 1994: 226)

As an African American writer who keenly sticks to the black culture and history, Morrison dedicates herself to incorporate this unique black cultural characteristic into her writing.

The Bluest Eye is Toni Morrison's first novel. The initial publication of this novel is like Pecola's life: dismissed, trivialized, misread. And it has taken twenty-five years for the novel to gain a respectful publication. It is a poignant story of racial discrimination which exposes the miserable life of an African American girl in the white-dominated society. Setting in Morrison's hometown, Lorain, Ohio, in 1941, the protagonist is an eleven-year-old African American girl named Pecola Breedlove. Pecola longs to have a pair of blue eyes like the white girls. She lives in a black community where she is considered as an ugly child by people surrounding her. She is maltreated and discriminated against by almost everyone in her life including her parents. Pecola attributes her frustrating life to her black skin and wishes for a pair of blue eyes which would make her beautiful. However, she is finally driven insane and hallucinates that she has been granted the blue eyes.

This novel was completed within five years, Morrison once stated that she focused on how something as grotesque as racial discrimination could affect the inner world of the most delicate member of society: a child and the most vulnerable member—a female. In an interview in 1980, Morrison commented that her motive in *The Bluest Eye* was to write about the marginalized little girl who had never before been seriously treated by anyone in the literature (Taylor-Guthrie, 1994: 88). As Linden Peach examined, "It was the first novel to give a black child center stage; previously, the black child had not only been peripheral but doubly marginalized as a comic figure." (Peach, 1998: 7) Before its publication, only negative images of black children and black people were portrayed in white fictions. So this novel is a breakthrough to take a black girl as protagonist, which has a symbolic meaning in black literature.

Sula was written when the second-wave feminism swept the world in 1973. Feminists fought for equal rights against the male counterpart in the male-centered society. The length of the novel is short, but the social problem revealed in the novel is very sharp and big. It has created a new African American female image represented by Sula. That is quite different from the images described in former African American writers' works. Sula has an independent spirit and contempt the existing old-fashioned patterns of female family life. She leads her life unrestrained by the existing social custom to show her resistance to the unjust society. However, her radical independence leads her to conflict with others and alienates herself from the black community. Sula finally dies alone in the novel. *Sula* is subversive mainly from the perspective of gender and has a deeper insight into the life of African American women. To some extent, *Sula* is the continuation of *The Bluest Eye*. Morrison stated in her 1983 interview that both *The Bluest Eye* and *Sula* started from the childhood of the characters (Taylor-Guthrie, 1994: 163). If Pecola destroys herself with the values of superior white culture, then Sula, as her sharp confrontation of the conventions, revolts against male-dominated society by indulging in unrestrained sexuality.

Unlike other women living in Medallion, Sula violates the conventional rules and regulations in the black community. She refuses to marry and despises traditional social morality. She has sex with different townsmen, including the husband of her best friend, Nel. She goes to church without underwear and sends her grandmother to the old folk home. All her behaviors are considered as "witch" or "devil" in community. However, Sula insists on her lifestyle which is condemned by others and never regrets her choice. In the novel, Morrison shows that Sula's destructive lifestyle changes the indifferent and isolated black community to a close-related group. The townspeople have restored the long-lost virtues; they "protect and love each other. They begin to cherish their husbands and wives, protect their children, repair their homes, and in a general band together against the devil in their midst" (*Sula,* 117-118). Unfortunately, after Sula's death, the community is once again back to disintegration and extinguished in 1965 when the society underwent tremendous changes.

In *Sula*, Morrison changes her emphasis from African American women's victimization to resistance. An aggressive African American female image created by Morrison as Sula is no longer subject to the mainstream of American culture mixed with the white American culture and the black culture. In her third novel, *Song of Solomon* (1977), Morrison continues to explore the theme of self-searching and self-growth, the only difference is that she takes an African American male as protagonist this time. In her interview with Taylor-Guthrie, Morrison summarizes the momentum of writing her first three novels:

> But I think I still write about the same thing, which is about how people relate to one another and miss it or hang on to it—or are tenacious about love. —And about love and how to survive not to make a living—but how to survive whole in a world where we are all of us, in some measure, victims of something. Each one of us is in some way at some moment a victim and in no position to do a thing about it. Some child is always left unpicked up at

some moment. In a world like that, how does one remain whole—is it just possible to do that? (Taylor-Guthrie, 1994: 40)

The first three novels all focus on the recognition of an individual in a white-dominated society. Here Morrison draws on the black myth of flying as a method of Milkman's discovery of his ancestral roots in the southern area. Milkman's quest for gold, grandfather, ancestor, and the black culture in the south is the process of searching for cultural roots and identifying himself as an African American. During the process, he gradually gets rid of the bondage of material desire and realizes his spiritual and moral improvement, which finally helps him to discover the true meaning of living in the world. He has transferred from an indifferent, irresponsible, and ruthless person to an understanding, generous and grateful person. He learns to love people, to cherish the black culture and heritage, and to understand the black women's sacrifice through his adventurous quest. At last, Milkman finds the root of his ancestors and the black culture, finally completing the process of his self-growth. The publication of *Song of Solomon* is a sign that Morrison's writing has begun to mature. Morrison won the National Book Critics' Circle award after the publication of this novel and became one of the greatest contemporary American writers.

Tar Baby (1981), Morrison's fourth novel, was published in 1981, from which she steps into her second stage of writing. The novel tells a story of two young African American people who are attracted to each other but separated for their conflicting values. In this novel, Jadine goes to college in Paris with the financial assistance of Valerian, her uncle's white employer. She gains a sense of superiority and accomplishment over other African Americans with her success of being the cover girl of a famous fashion magazine in Paris. With higher education and immersion of the white culture and values, Jadine has alienated herself from the black culture and sticks to the pursuit of existence in the white-dominated society. She has become the slave of the white culture without her own cultural identity, which ends with the failure of her self-growth at last.

Son Green, who is Jadine's lover, sticks to the black traditional culture and values. Morrison uses the name of "Son" to symbolize that he is the son of the black culture and heritage. In Son's eyes, the best place to live in is the black community, which is full of virtues of love, cooperation, generosity, and equality. Son regards Paris, the white-dominated city, as an evil place for living. These two young people with different values are attracted to each other and later rent an apartment and live together in New York. However, their respective cultures turn into quarrels and fights with each other. Each wants to get rid of the restraint from the alien culture of each other. Their relationship breaks off when they leave New York, which is foreseen by their cultural conflicts. Through *Tar Baby*, Morrison suggests the possibility of a combination of the black and the white culture in an appropriate way, with the premise of adhering to one's own culture. Without an effective infusion, both Jadine and Son fail to achieve their self-achievement. In Morrison's next novel, *Beloved*, we can see the success of constructing self-identity even it is accomplished with tremendous hardships.

Morrison's fifth novel, *Beloved* (1987) is a wonderful presentation of African American women's fight against racism and sexism, and it is considered as the best work of Morrison. Since its publication, *Beloved* has received high praise in the literary world as "the milestone in the history of American literature". *Chicago Sun-Times* once valued it as "Toni Morrison's finest work ... Nothing she has written so sets her apart, so displays her prodigious, almost shocking talent". *Beloved* won the Pulitzer Prize in Fiction, the Robert F. Kennedy Book Award, and the Melcher Book Award. The novel is based on a real story. When Morrison was editing *The Black Book* at Random House, she read a newspaper article about a fugitive slave woman named Margaret Garner. When Margaret and her four children were in danger of being captured by the white slave owner, she decided to kill her children and then committed suicide to prevent them from being slaves again. However, she only succeeded in killing one of her daughters before she was captured by a slave owner. Morrison was deeply shocked by this story and developed it into *Beloved* to show the cruelty of slavery. Morrison spent two years on composing the novel and three years on writing. The novel revealed the darkest period of the slavery system in American history and the physical and mental destruction brought by slavery on black people.

The novel is set after the Civil War (1861-1865), during the period of Reconstruction. The protagonist, Sethe lives in 124 House with her daughter Denver. The house has been haunted by the ghost of a child for eighteen years. In 1855, Sethe is a slave in Sweet Home. She and her children escape from Sweet Home to 124 House because of the cruel treatment of the slave owner. They only enjoy twenty-eight days of freedom before the white owner comes to catch them. To prevent her children from being slaves again, Sethe cuts the throat of her two-year-old daughter. Eighteen years after the abolition of slavery, Sethe is spiritually tormented by the infanticide. In her new house in Ohio, she is continually haunted by the ghost of the baby girl named Beloved. Sethe believes that Beloved is the incarnation of her daughter's ghost; she tries to do everything to satisfy the girl's requirements. It is her daughter, Denver, who steps out to the black community to ask for help. Finally, people in the black community exorcise the ghost out of the house and Sethe is saved. *Beloved* shows us a cruel history of slavery during which African Americans have endured physical, emotional, sexual, and spiritual sufferings. In *Beloved*, Morrison describes a distorted maternal love expressed by Sethe with violence. While *Beloved* deals with the love between mother and daughter, the next two novels, *Jazz* (1992) and *Paradise* (1998) discuss different aspects of love in human society, which constitute Morrison's "trilogy of love" together with *Beloved*.

Published in 1992, *Jazz* unwinds the narration and develops the story plots employing improvisation of jazz music. The background of the story is in the 1920s, describing the life of a middle-aged couple in Harlem District, New York City. Joe and Violet escape from the southern countryside to the northern city. Joe lives on selling cosmetics and Violet is a hairdresser. Living in the discriminated white-dominated city, they gradually loss their inner tranquility. Their estrangement from each other leads to Joe's affair with a young girl named Dorcas. When Joe finds that Dorcas is dating another man, Joe shoots her dead. Violet goes to Dorcas' funeral with a knife trying to cut the dead girl's face out of hatred. This love triangle causes Dorcas' death and brings misery to Joe and Violet as well. In this novel, there is a character named Felice, who is Dorcas' close friend. She helps Joe free from grief by telling him Dorcas' true love. As for Violet, with the help of Dorcas' aunt, Alice, she learns the meaning of love and understanding between spouses. Fortunately, Joe and Violet break the ice between them and start to communicate with each other. With mutual understanding and forgiveness, they restore their love once again. In *Jazz*, Morrison depicts the difficult process of the southern African Americans' adjustments to live in the northern cities in the 1920s. She shows the indifference, estrangement, and even hostility caused by the lack of communication within family and community between people, especially between husband and wife.

Paradise (1998) is Morrison's seventh novel. It mainly focuses on the history and development of the black race. Racism is the main subject of Morrison's criticism, and she also objects to the radical Black Nationalism. The novel is based on a story Morrison heard while on a trip to Brazil in the 1980s. It is about the Convent women who are murdered by a group of African American men in the town of Ruby. The reason behind the murder is these women have challenged their male power and authority in the black community.

Morrison sets the story in a rarely-known town of Ruby in Oklahoma, where there is a large African American population. The other location of the shooting is Convent, which is seventeen miles away from Ruby. It is a refuge for the deserted or traumatized women. Ruby is named after the sister of the Morgan twins who are in charge of Ruby Town. They attempt to retain the purity of their community and stay away from the white people. Convent is not far away from Ruby. It is charged by Consolata who accepts wandering and homeless women and gives them help regardless of race, gender, or skin difference. As the story continues, the women in Ruby find consolation from the Convent woman and gradually form a close relationship with them. However, in the eyes of Ruby men, the alliance between Ruby women and Convent women poses a mortal threat to their patriarchal power. Those Ruby women have deviated from ideal images bestowed by men. They are considered as a threat to the male-dominated community. They blame the Convent women and rush into Convent, murdering five women for fear of losing control over them. Morrison's previous novels are set in the black community and describe only a few individuals specifically. However, *Paradise* is set in Ruby Town and Convent with scores of characters telling their own stories. Morrison once redefined "paradise" as the concept of taking God's chosen people and alienating them from others.

In 2003, when Morrison published *Love*, critics argued that it repeated the themes of Morrison's former novels, such as the bond between women and mother-daughter relation. Scholars Wang and Wu state as follows:

> In terms of theme, *Love* can be traced back to the same origin with Morrison's former love trilogy of *Beloved* (about maternal love), *Jazz* (about lovers' love) and *Paradise* (about religious love) as has been aforementioned, all of which place a high premium on the importance of communication. (Wang ,Wu, 1997: 201)

What is more important is that Morrison deals with different kinds of love in her novels as Wang and Wu say in the above citation. In this novel, Morrison narrates the story of a group of women in the Cosey family. The narrator of this story is a woman named L, who is the chef at a seaside resort owned by the Cosey family. In this story, only the descendants of Bill Cosey are alive, including his grand-daughter Christine and his second wife Heed, these two girls are best friends at the very beginning of the story. Heed was 11 years old when Cosey bought her as his second wife. From then on, Cosey's daughter-in-law, May, does whatever she can to keep Christine away from Heed because of jealousy. In the Cosey family, there are endless conflicts and battles between these women even after Cosey's death. Christine and Heed live in the same house but on separate floors, which symbolizes the obstacles between these two girls. They consider each other as an enemy to contend for Cosey's love and affection, and ultimately develop a deep hatred for each other. Fortunately, with the efforts of L, Christine and Heed begin to understand their predicament and miseries in the male-dominated family. They realize that African American women have nobody but themselves to rely on and restore their friendship at the end of the novel. By describing the final harmonious relationship between Heed and Christine, Morrison demonstrates the importance of the unity of African American women.

In *Love*, Morrison ponders over how love can change the destinies of women. Ever since Morrison enters her third stage of writing, she begins to depict African American women in the community rather than being isolated from the community in some way. Morrison's ninth novel, *A Mercy* (2008) depicts the living conditions of females of different races in 17th century America. The novel is set in the 1680s in American colonies. Morrison writes the story that Jacob collects laborers of different ethnic groups, including Portuguese, Dutch, English, Native American, African, and mixed-race people. Morrison extends the concept of slavery to everyone and shows that servitude has little to do with skin color. At the very beginning of the novel, all ethnic groups work together with Jacob, trying to build their family with respect and happiness like a paradise. Unfortunately, the white master begins the excessive pursuit of extravagance and money, which finally leads to the degradation of the family and his death. After his death, racial violence begins to appear. The paradise turns into a lost paradise at last. With the purpose of reconstructing a paradise again, Morrison depicts Florens' awakening journey, Sorrow's rebirth, and Lina's return to Indian to show that ethnic groups can work together to reconstruct a harmonious homeland. It shows Morrison's expectation of constructing a paradise that all ethnic groups can share and live harmoniously with each other.

Home, which was published in 2012, is Toni Morrison's tenth novel. Compared to her former novels, it is short and only 146 pages long. The background of this novel is set in the 1950s when racism and McCarthyism prevailed around the country. This novel tells a story of a defeated African American veteran Frank Money, who finds his manhood and spiritual home by saving his sister from the edge of death. He lives an aimless and crazy life in a northern city after coming back from the battlefield. Frank is reluctant to go back to his hometown, Lotus, because of his terrible childhood memories. However, he receives a letter saying that her sister, Cee, is on the edge of death in Atlanta. Frank goes to Atlanta to bring Cee back to their hometown at last. With the help of people in the community, Frank and Cee successfully overcome their traumas, establish their self-identity, and set up a stable life there. Although the journey home is full of hardships and danger, their physical and psychological traumas are finally resolved with the sense of belonging. And they regain the courage to undertake responsibilities. In this novel, Morrison expresses a positive and optimistic view of African Americans' future.

God Help the Child, published in 2015, is Morrison's latest work. Unlike her former novels, the story is set in the background of current American society. In the novel, Morrison explores how different races, genders, classes work together in modern American society despite historical traumas. It is divided into three parts with seventeen chapters, of which fourteen chapters are named after different narrators' names with a first-person perspective. The story revolves around a successful cosmetics designer named Bride, who is born with stunning black skin. Because of her skin color, Bride's mother forbids her to call mother and her father abandons her ruthlessly. Bride grows up without her parents' love and cares. She starts her new life after following the advice of Jeri, a designer, to wear white clothes only, which makes her successful in the fashion industry. Booker, who is Bride's lover and soul mate, helps Bride to confront her childhood trauma bravely. There are misunderstanding and conflict between them throughout the novel. By the end of the novel, as the misunderstanding is clarified, Bride and Booker finally become reconciled. Morrison depicts Bride's process to retrieve her true love for Booker with courage. The novel ends up with the words of Bride's mother, who takes a lifetime to understand "what you do to children matters" and blesses Bride's child with "God help the child". In this novel, Morrison shows that love, understanding, and tolerance are the most powerful instruments to dismiss the conflict caused by racial discrimination, sexism, and alienation of family members, child abuse, and other problems existing in society.

With outstanding literary talent and extraordinary imagination, Morrison completes eleven novels during her lifetime. The first four novels mainly explore the evil impact of the white culture and beauty standards on African Americans, especially on African American women and children. During this period, African American women's struggle for independence and equality is the main concern of Morrison's works. From the fifth novel, *Beloved*, Morrison begins to consider the situation of her race in the white society. At this stage, Morrison not only blames white culture as the cause of the suffering of African Americans but also reflects on the problems existing between themselves. After entering the 21st century, Morrison switches her focus to explore the problems of humanity in a broad sense in her later novels such as *A Mercy* and *God Help the Child*. Morrison's great success in the literary field has attracted the attention from readers and critics all around the world. The following part focuses on previous studies that have been done by researchers and critics on Morrison's literary works.

1.2 Literature Review

Morrison began her literary career as a novelist in the second half of the 20th century when various critical theories flourished. The overall evaluation and interpretation of her works have been diversified. In general, research results can be divided into three categories from the perspective of research objects. The first category is the general study of Morrison and her works, such as her life, statements, and thoughts. The second category is the case study of one or more than one of her works. And the last category is the comparative studies which compare Morrison with other writers.

Many scholars study Morrison's works from different perspectives with various literary critical methods. Western scholars start to study Morrison's works from the late 1970s on her literary thoughts and writing style. In 1976, the first critical book by Barbara Smith, *American Black Feminism Study* was published. It was an extensive research on Toni Morrison's works. Then Robert Stepto published his interview with Toni Morrison on *Melus* in 1977, and Jane Bakerman published her interview with Toni Morrison on *Black American Literature Forum* in 1978. By the end of the 1980s, Morrison had published 5 novels in succession. Racial study, gender criticism, and class issues have been critics' main critical perspectives. *The World of Toni Morrison: Explorations in Literary Criticism* (1985) by Bessie W. Jones and Andrey L. Vinson, explores many different topics related to Toni Morrison's works.

Kalla F. C. Hollyway published her work *New Dimensions of Spiritually: A Biracial and Bicultural Reading of the Novels of Toni Morrison* (1987), focusing on the severe trauma that African Americans endured in the white-dominated society. In 1988, Nellie Y. Mckay published *Critical Essays on Toni Morrison* (1988), which introduces Morrison's life, works, and main thoughts systematically. Harold Bloom's book, *Toni Morrison* (1990), composes of 11 critical essays on Toni Morrison together with Morrison's critical paper. In *The Voice of Toni Morrison* (1991), Barbara Hill Rigney mainly analyzes the racial, social, and gender inequality of African Americans in America. Susan Snider Lanser, in her *Fictions of Authority: Women Writers and Narrative Voice* (1992), probes into the change of narrative voice in Morrison's first five novels from *The Bluest Eye* to *Beloved*.

After winning the Nobel Prize in Literature, Morrison's works have been accepted and analyzed broadly by more and more literary critics. She has become the most famous contemporary African American female writer in the field of American literature. Studies on Morrison mainly focus on her reconstruction of black history and interpretation of the relationship between history, memory, community, and trauma. For instance, Hazel V. Carby's *Reconstructing Womanhood: The Emergence of the Afro-American Woman Novelist* (1992) and Carole B. Davis' *Black Women: Writing and Identity: Migration of the Subject* (2002), both of them analyze the new African American female images with independent self-consciousness in Morrison's works. *A World of Difference: An Inter-Cultural Study of Toni Morrison's Novels* (1994), written by Wendy Harding and Jacky Martin, is concerned with the modes of belongings within the black community. They also study other aspects of the community, such as its origin, function, and the way it is represented in the novels. *The Novels of Toni Morrison: The Search for Self and Place Within the Community* (1996) by Patrick Bryce Bjork, pays attention to the relationship between community and individual in Morrison's first five novels, and contends that individual can't find their self-identity without the black community. What is more, Gurleen Grewal examines Morrison's works from the perspectives of race, gender, culture, and class in *Circles of Sorrow, Lines of Struggle: The Novels of Toni Morrison* (1998). In *Religiosity, Cosmology, and Folklore: The African Influence in the Novels of Toni Morrison* (2001), Therese E. Higgins studies the influence of the black community and analyzes the African cultural elements in Morrison's novels. In *Toni Morrison's Developing Class Consciousness* (1991), Doreatha Drummond Mbalia studies the class consciousness and relations between black Americans and white Americans in Morrison's works. Jennifer Lee Jordan Heiner analyzes Morrison's narrative strategies and makes a contrast with the traditional literary form in her *Narrative Conventions and Race in the Novels of Toni Morrison* (2008). Jordan thinks that Morrison subverts the traditional narrative logic that has been imposed by the white-dominated narrative theory. The author classifies and summarizes the monographes on Morrison according to the periods, which provides multiple research perspectives for the interpretation of Morrison's works.

The research on Morrison's works can also be divided into several aspects in terms of themes and critical methods. Critical methods mainly include feminist criticism, racist criticism, black cultural study, trauma study, post-colonial criticism, comparative study, and narrative study.

Feminist criticism is the most popular and earliest perspective that is applied to study Morrison's works. Barbara Rigney Hill applies feminist deconstructionist in her essay "Hagar's Mirror: Self and Identity in Morrison's Fictions" (1991) regarding Morrison's novels *Beloved*, *The Bluest Eye,* and *Sula*. In the essay, Rigney argues that Morrison's work is distinguished by reformations of self, identity, and history. Carole B. Davis in his *Black Women: Writing Identity: Migration of the Subject* (2002) explores a complex and fascinating set of interrelated issues including gender, heritage, and identity. He also examines African American woman's resistance to white domination. In *Toni Morrison and Womanish Discourse* (1999), Mori Aoi applies feminism to explain how Morrison returns to her African American identity and finds her own artistically form. In "The Convergence of Feminism and Ethnicity in the Fiction of Toni Morrison" (1988), Carolyn Denard explores the damages of sexist oppression within and without ethnic group to African American woman. In "Black Feminism: What Women of Color Went Through in Toni Morrison's Selected Novels" (2015), Ayda Rahmani describes the helplessness and pain of African American women in *The Bluest Eye* and *Beloved* from the perspective of black feminism.

Racial issue has frequently been the core of Morrison's works and the focus of many critics. Trudier Harris, in his *Fiction and Folklore* (1991), demonstrates that all of Morrison's concerns are based on African-American folk tradition. Harris argues that Morrison tries to situate her works in the whole of folk aura.

Ritashona Simpson in *Black Looks & Black Acts* (2007) discusses Morrison's dedication to the written black language used to represent the black race. Tadd Ruetenik's essay "Animal Liberation or Human Redemption: Racism and Speciesism in Toni Morrison's *Beloved*" (2010), is an exploration of a morally sophisticated slave narrative that deals with the topic of racism in American historical consciousness. In "The Furrow of His Brow: Providence and Pragmatism in Toni Morrison's *Paradise*" (2012), Amy Fuqua explores the racial issues in *Paradise* and *A Mercy* from the point of the American myth of exceptionalism.

As to the historical and cultural trauma, in *Race, Trauma, and Home* (2009), Evelyn Jaffe Schreiber puts forward the concepts of "home". It is a physical place, community or relationship, which is reconstructed through memory to serve as a healing space for Morrison's characters to reconstruct self-identity. In *Spectrality in the Novels of Toni Morrison* (2013), Melanie R. Anderson points out that Morrison organizes her novels with cultural history in mind. She says that Morrison's works are consisted of preoccupation with spectrality and the haunting disjointed natures of both personal and cultural history. She argues that these "ghosted characters" are racial memories, which continue to haunt the present life of characters. Religion is also an important aspect of Morrison's study. Jeannette King's "Paradise Lost and Regained: Toni Morrison and Alice Walker" (2000) states that novels of Toni Morrison and Alice Walker have consistently acknowledged the revolutionary potential of Christian discourse as a form of liberation for African American women. Jeanna Fuston White in his essay "Two Vashtis: Morrison's *Beloved* and *The Book of Esther*" (2013), discusses the intertextuality between *Beloved* and the story of Vashtis in *The Book of Esther*. Sima Farshid in "The Crucial Role of Naming in Toni Morrison's *Song of Solomon*" (2015) discusses the importance of biblical names in *Song of Solomon*.

Critics make in-depth studies on Morrison's works from the perspective of cultural criticism. And the relationship between community and individual is one of the focuses of discussion. In "The Burden of Liberty: Choice in Toni Morrison's

Jazz and Toni Cade Barbara's *The Salt Eaters*" (1996), Derek Alwes argues that Joe and Violet do those things out of the liberty they acquired in the black community in the northern city. In "Toni Morrison's *Jazz* and the City" (2001), Anne-Marie Paquet-Deyris thinks that Joe and Violet's tragedy results from a sense of displacement after they come to the northern city. Cultural identity and identification studies are one of the frequently discussed topics in postcolonial criticism. "Reconnecting Fragments: Afro-American Folk Tradition in *The Bluest Eye*" (1988) by Trudier Harris studies the folk culture of the black community in the novel. He says that beneath the specifics of folk culture is a caring which is a life-sustaining force to African Americans. And it is the absence of this force in Lorain that results in Pecola's tragedy.

Some critics investigate Morrison's novels with narrative criticism, including narrative structure, narrative strategy, and narrative discourse, etc. Such as Rob Davidson's "Racial Stock and 8-Rocks: Communal Historiography in Toni Morrison's *Paradise*" (2001). It analyses how Morrison constructs the social characteristics in *Paradise* through narration. Critical approaches applied to read and appreciate Morrison's novels are quite diverse and extensive. In this book, the author reads Toni Morrison's novels with Confucianism, which is a relatively new perspective. In the following part, significance of this study and research methods are introduced.

1.3 Significance and Methods

From the literary review, we can see that a lot of scholars have studied Toni Morrison's novels from various perspectives and many achievements have been made. However, there is no research has been done from the perspective of Confucianism. The reason why the author studies her novels from Confucianism lies in the fact that Morrison has a connection to Confucianism. There are evidences to show that Confucianism has some influence on Morrison's writing.

When Jiao Xiaoting interviewed Toni Morrison in 2015, Morrison said she has been to China in 1984 with her younger son and other 6 American writers, along with Maxine Hong Kingston (Tang Tingting). (Jiao, 2016: 4). They were invited as guests of China Writers Association, where these writers exchanged literary ideas with each other. During her visit to China, Morrison experienced the reality of Chinese people's life based on Confucianism. Kingston described her first trip to China in the *Biographical Dictionary of Chinese Women* as follows:

> It was a first trip to China. As a guest of China Writers Association; and I traveled with seven other writers, including Toni Morrison, Allen Ginsberg, and Gary Snyder, visiting my native village and meeting some of my relatives for the first time. (Honglee, 2003: 281)

Kingston is a Chinese American writer, and a friend of Morrison to some extent due to their similar identities of ethnic minority writers in America. During the late 1980s, Kingston's works "has been dismissed as Orientalist" (Honglee, 2003: 282). As Morrison and Kingston have been literary friends for a long time, it is natural that they influence each other on their thoughts. Even though Morrison visited China in the 1980s, she has some inclination to Chinese philosophy before.

Her experience as an editor at Random House leads her to learn eastern philosophy. *The Analects of Confucius—A Philosophical Translation* was published by Random House. This book provides readers with a new perspective on the central canonical text that has defined Chinese culture and clearly illuminates the spirit and values of Confucius. And Jeffery Moses published her book *Oneness* by Random House. As Morrison worked for Random House, it is sure that her working experience in Random House gave her convenience to learn the gist of Confucianism and other Eastern philosophy.

Studying the development of Confucianism in America, the author found Morrison was greatly influenced by Ralph Waldo Emerson (1803–1882). Emerson led the transcendentalist movement of the mid-19th century in America. He endowed Confucius with great honor and showed his respect and admiration for Confucius. Emerson quoted the *Sayings of Confucius and Mencius* as illustrations of his ideas. Kyle Bryant Simmons published *Emerson, the American Confucius* in 2013. This book contextualizes Emerson's application and appreciation of Confucian motifs and quotations in his journals, sermons, lectures, and publications from 1832 onward. Mathew A. Foust in *Confucianism and American Philosophy* states the connection between Emerson and Confucianism, "Excerpts for Emerson's journals dated March 3, 1836, feature dozens of sentences of Confucius" (Foust, 1997:19). Foust argues, Emerson and Confucius find common ground in the capacity of friends to promote mutual moral cultivation. Confucianism provides an indispensable ideological material for his literary writing.

Lots of scholars prove that Morrison's writing is greatly influenced by Emerson. In "Pain and Unmaking of Self in Toni Morrison's *Beloved*", Kristin Boudreau points out Morrison's process of self-identity construction as a real fully human is much like Emerson's ideas of "courting suffering in order to verify our humanity" (Boudreau, 2001:464). Jerry A. Varsava says in an article "Review: The Dialectics of Self and Community in Toni Morrison and Thomas Pynchon", Emersonian liberalism, which emphasizes variously, self-reliance, personal willpower, and nonconformity, has demonstrated in Morrison's works. Varsava (2002:796) says, "In Emerson's own case, he promoted the liberation of enslaved African Americans in what is a hallmark example of the liberal's respect for the broader polity." Since Emerson is an "American Confucius", Morrison's close relationship with him made her learn Confucianism through him.

Apart from Ralph Waldo Emerson, another philosopher of transcendentalism, Henry David Thoreau (1817–1862) also has a great influence on Morrison. His book *Walden* and his essay "Civil Disobedience" are interwoven with close observation of nature, personal experience, pointed rhetoric, symbolic meanings, and historical lore. Thoreau also advocated abandoning waste and illusion in order to discover life's true essential needs. Chinese philosophy, specifically Confucianism has influenced Thoreau's writings and thoughts. In *Thoreau's Quotations from the Confucian Books* (1961), Lyman V. Cady theorizes that the vast majority of the Confucian quotations that appear in Thoreau's *Walden*. In *Confucianism and American Philosophy,* Mathew A. Foust focuses on Thoreau's political thought as expressed in his seminal essay "Civil Disobedience". In this essay Thoreau refers to *The Analects* and *Mencius*. Confucianism has had a large effect on the structure or themes present in Thoreau's work. In "The Wild Ones, Society's Response to Social Deviants", Danielle Penick holds that Thoreau's presentation of struggle that occur between the individual and society are clearly evident in the works of Toni Morrison. In *Walden*, Thoreau argues that "excess materialistic ownership or taste, whether it is shelter, clothing, or food, was a shackle to enslave oneself instead of emancipation". Thoreau's thought of the damaging impact from a consumer culture is displayed in Morrison's works as well. There is more evidence to show Morrison's writing and thought has been influenced by Thoreau's philosophy which related to Confucianism.

From what examined above, lots of critics proved that Morrison was influenced by Confucianism on her thoughts and writing. Even though the author didn't check other pieces of evidence such as her letters with her friends, her curriculum in the university days, her books in her library, with the help of lots of scholars, it is sure that she learned Confucianism or that she at least got influenced by Confucianism through her job as an editor of Random House and two famous transcendentalists Emerson and Thoreau. The fact that Morrison's profound views on interrelationships, such as race relations, gender relations, familial relations, and relations between nature and humans have a lot in common with Confucianism is the most convincing proof that she was influenced by Confucianism.

Confucianism is a very broad idea and a systematic philosophy. It can be applied to everything, for example, how to live, how to behave, how to rule the country, the way of the emperor, etc. The author here focuses on the thought of "unity of Heaven and human", which deals with the relationship between human and nature, human and society, and human with the inner self. Through reading Morrison's novels, the author finds that many ideas expressed in her works are corresponding with the ideas of Confucian "unity of Heaven and human". So far, there is not yet any criticism that has discussed Morrison's novels from the perspective of Confucianism. This book aims at preceding a comprehensive study on Morrison's novels with Confucianism, which helps us understand her works and thoughts more deeply.

The research methods adopted in this book include document analysis and text analysis. In the stage of document collecting, the author makes full use of network resources to find the literary research materials related to Morrison's novels. By classifying and sorting the materials, the author finishes the literary review section. In the process of writing the main body of the book, text analysis method is used to mark content that relevant to Confucian "unity of Heaven and human" in Morrison's novels. This book takes the three main ideas of "unity of Heaven and human" as three dimensions to study Morrison's works. The author expounds systematically on the embodiment of Confucian "unity of Heaven and human" in Morrison's works. A brief introduction of the Confucian "unity of Heaven and human" is given in the following section.

1.4 Confucian "Unity of Heaven and Human"

China has more than five-thousand-year history of civilization. During its long history, it gradually forms a set of traditional philosophy, of which the relationship between Heaven and human has always been the focus of attention. Confucianism, as the core of Chinese traditional values, occupies a dominant position in Chinese traditional philosophy. And the thought of "unity of Heaven and human" (*tianren heyi*, 天人合一) in Confucianism contains rich ideological content. It mainly focuses on relations of Heaven, earth, and human. The aim of "unity of Heaven and human" is to achieve harmony and coexistence of Heaven and human, including the harmony of human and nature, human and society, human and the inner self. It is originated from the *Book of Changes,* and sprouted from Confucius who is the greatest Confucian philosopher in ancient China. It is then inherited and developed by Mencius and Xunzi and other Confucian scholars of the later dynasties into a systematic philosophy.

The thought of "unity of Heaven and human" originates from the *Book of Changes.* This book makes a philosophic abstraction and deduction of the universe, and regards Heaven, human, and nature as interactive organic from an overall perspective. It also puts forward a set of modes for the natural generation of Heaven and thinks the change of all things is promoted by *taiji* (the supreme ultimate). *Taiji* refers to the origin of the world. The ancient Chinese saw it either as *qi* (气, vital force) or *yuanqi* (元气, primordial vital force) that permeates the chaotic world. It is derived from Heaven and earth and devotes to the creation of all things, and finally completes the performance of the whole world. "Changes evolve from *taiji*, which gives rise to two primal forces of *yin* and *yang.* The two forces generate the four images, and the four images generate the eight trigrams." According to *Book of Changes*:

> There is Heaven and earth then there is everything, there is everything then there is man and woman, there are man and woman then there is a couple, there is a couple then there is father and son.

Hence, Heaven is the root of all life, without which all life is impossible in the universe. It is an orderly generation process from the root of the universe to all things, from nature to society. It forms a complete sequence in which Heaven, earth and human are closely connected. The cosmological theory of the *Book of Changes* lays an important theoretical foundation for the explanation of the relationship between Heaven and human. It sets up the universal formation chain of Heaven and earth, everything, man and woman, father and son, emphasizing that human is the son of Heaven. It holds the essence of Heaven, earth, and human is the same.

Heaven (*tian*, 天) is a sacred and fundamental concept in ancient Chinese philosophy. It has three different meanings. The first meaning is the physical sky or the entirety of nature (not including human society), the operations of which manifest certain laws and order. The second meaning refers to a spiritual being, which possesses an anthropomorphic will and governs everything in the universe. The third meaning denotes the universal law, which is observed by all things and beings. It is also the basis of human nature, morality, social and political orders. "Heaven" also means *di* (帝), which is respected by the Chinese nation at the beginning of the culture. It reflects the hazy knowledge of nature and human, and they ascribe the reason for the inexplicable phenomena of nature and society to the will of *di* (帝). In ancient times, people believed that there was a mysterious power behind natural phenomena when facing the changeable and unpredictable nature. Human activities were subject to its control and became slaves of Heaven. The concept of "unity of Heaven and human" was first conceived in the soil of agricultural civilization. During that time, human can't explain the natural phenomena, and was curious about the unknowing things of nature. They thought that smooth progress of agricultural production depended not only on human labor but also on natural conditions and environment. As a result, Heaven and earth were endowed with mysterious colors and personal emotions. Human beings regarded Heaven with great awe because nature can deliver its praises and warnings to them through different kinds of auspicious or disastrous natural phenomena.

During the three dynasties of Xia, Shang, and Zhou, "Heaven" was regarded as the supreme personified God. It was generally believed that Heaven governs all things in the universe, social phenomena, and human destiny. The process of Heaven generating things is:

Providence is unique, from which produces the Positive and Negative Forces, the Positive and Negative Forces intersect to produce a third party then there are the things in the world. Everything contains the Positive and Negative Forces; they interact with each other to achieve harmony and unity. (Lao Tzu, 1999: 44)

Heaven was endowed with the will of human beings. Rulers of the Zhou Dynasty insisted that the king was appointed by Heaven on earth with great virtues. And the royal power represented the will of divine power of Heaven; to obey the royal power was to obey the divine power. In this way, Heaven was endowed with moral character. It was a kind of wholehearted worship of human toward Heaven, believing that Heaven had complete control over human life and fate. It had established a basic framework to study the relationship between Heaven and human in ancient China during the Pre-Qin period.

The early concept of "unity of Heaven and human" can be divided into two periods: before and after the Spring and Autumn period. Before it belonged to the religious theology category, and after that belonged to the philosophy category. In the late Spring and Autumn period, Confucius expounded on the relationship between Heaven and human from the perspective of life philosophy. Confucius's exposition on Heaven opened an essential understanding of the relationship between Heaven and human. He regards Heaven as the creator in charge of the operation of all things. He holds the alternation of four seasons and the birth of all things were all due to Heaven. Confucius emphasizes that human should follow the Way of Heaven, otherwise would be punished by Heaven. "He who offends against Heaven has none to whom he can pray." (Annping, 2014: 66) Confucius also believes that the Way of heaven is the source or the basis of human's moral conduct and orderly human relations. One should comply with the Way of Heaven in both words and deeds, as well as with human relations. Human should recognize and develop the moral nature bestowed upon by Heaven to gain access to the Way of Heaven. Moreover, human beings need to practice humanity according to the Way of Heaven to achieve the unity of Heaven and human. Here, Confucius' humanity refers to ethics and virtues of human beings, which can only be achieved through "benevolence".

As to the destiny of human beings, Confucius claims that it is decided by Heaven, which shows his reverence to Heaven. Just like he said, "There are three things of which the superior man stands in awe. He stands in awe of the decree of Heaven. He stands in awe of a great man. He stands in awe of the words of sages." (Annping, 2014: 319) Confucius enriched the definition of Heaven in the Western Zhou Dynasty and endowed it with human nature, likewise "Heaven produced the virtue that is in me" (Annping, 2014:144) and "It is Heaven that knows me" (Annping, 2014: 283). Confucius' view is that "man can be juxtaposed with Heaven and Earth" (B. Yang, 1993: 48). Although Confucius' view retains the mysterious thought of destiny; the essence is to emphasize the ethical significance of social norms and human behaviors. He advocates to practice humanity with benevolence to reach the Way of Heaven.

Mencius, as the main representative figure of Confucianism after Confucius, inherits and develops the Confucian "unity of Heaven and human". He claims that human nature and the nature of Heaven are fundamentally the same. And Mencius retains the moral concern of Heaven's Mandate (*tian ming*, 天命) but speaking of *ming* (命, mandate, decree) more abstractly. For Mencius, *ming* refers to the conditions of life that are beyond human control—what is simply "given". The realm of *ming* includes the brutal faces of our lives, such as where, when, and to whom we are born. It determines some of the parameters or limiting conditions within which our lives unfold. From the perspective of the individual, *ming* is the realm of necessity, which we can't control. Mencius states that human nature (*xing*, 性) is also given or endowed by Heaven, but the goodness of human nature is given only in potential form, as certain moral feelings or dispositions. So *xing*, for Mencius, concerns an area of life over which we do have some control. Mencius holds the view in *Mencius*:

> Nature is what Heaven has endowed. Therefore, he who exerts his mind (heart) to the utmost knows his nature. He who knows his nature knows Heaven. To preserve one's mind (heart) and to nourish one's nature is the way to serve Heaven.

Mencius means that person who knows his nature can serve Heaven by cultivating the nobility of Heaven, which is the well-known principle of Heaven-man unity in Chinese philosophy.

Mencius thinks Heaven is usually a naturalistic term, yet still with a moral dimension. It is the source of the cosmic order (*li*, 理) and the moral order (*daoli*, 道理). For a human being, one's nature is the instantiation of that order. The good nature given by Heaven that Mencius has discussed is now called more specifically "the nature of Heaven-and-earth" (*tiandi zhi xing*, 天地之性) or the "original nature" (*ben xing*, 本性). Mencius thinks that Heaven produces all things, and human beings and all things are originated from the same source. Both of them are an integral part of Heaven. Mencius extends the Confucian idea of benevolence from the love of close relatives to other people and eventually to all things in the world in *Mencius*:

> Men of virtue cherish all things but this is not benevolent love, have compassion for others but this is not the love of family. Men of virtue love and care for their loved ones, they are kind to other people. When they are kind to people, they treasure everything on earth.

Here, Mencius advocates that human beings should treat all things in the universe with love and benevolence. He connects human nature with Heaven and believes the essence of Heaven is the root of virtues of human beings. And the ethics of human beings is the embodiment of the essence of Heaven. Heaven and human are interlinked in nature and ethics. Humans can finally reach the unity of Heaven and human by observing human nature to seek a true understanding of the nature of Heaven. Mencius is famous for developing Confucianism into a big school of philosophy. Thanks to his effort, Confucianism gets an everlasting status in Chinese philosophy.

In the relationship between Heaven and human, Xunzi, an inheritor of Confucianism, puts forward the idea of "distinction between human and Heaven" (*tianren xiangfen*, 天人相分). This term holds that Heaven and human are different. Xunzi argues that Heaven and human each has a different role and that they should not be mixed. Temporal changes of Heaven and earth as well as seasonal changes in temperature and rainfall all belong to the domain of Heaven. They have their normal path, unrelated to human affairs, and are beyond the reach of human power. On the other hand, humans' morality and order in the world belong to the realm of man. People should be responsible for moral development and social order. Only by making a clear distinction between Heaven and man could one develop his abilities on the basis established by Heaven, without over stepping into a domain where man is unable to exert his power. As Xunzi said:

> Heaven operates on consistent principles. These principles did not exist for the sake of Yao and did not die away for the sake of Jie. To respond to these principles with orderly governance brings fortune, to respond to these principles with chaos brings misfortune. If you strengthen agriculture and use resources sparingly, then Heaven cannot make you poor. If you take care of your body and take action at the appropriate times, Heaven cannot make you sick. If you cultivate your virtue and are not distracted from your goal, then Heaven cannot bring you to disaster. Therefore, he who understands the distinction between nature and man may be called the wisest man. (Wang, 1978: 8)

The essence of "distinction between human and Heaven" is to separate human from the objective world and to gain independence. The reason that Xunzi stresses the distinction between human and Heaven is that both have their laws, functions, and norms of existence. What's more, human can make use of Heaven for the benefit of mankind based on understanding the laws of Heaven. At the same time, human must overcome the unfavorable conditions of Heaven, which exactly constitutes a dialectical and unified relationship between Heaven and human. Xunzi's "distinction of human and Heaven" mainly emphasizes the subjective initiative of mankind. He believes that human can use the external environment to serve themselves.

From the understanding and exposition of the relationship between Heaven and human by Confucius, Mencius, and Xunzi, we can find that Confucianism in the Pre-Qin period advocates that Heaven is not the only decisive force in the universe. It also emphasizes the initiative of human beings. The essence is to affirm the unique value of human in the universe.

In the Han Dynasty, compared with human's mysterious worship of Heaven in the Pre-Qin period, the relationship between Heaven and human has been discussed systematically. One of the most eminent Confucian scholars of this period is Dong Zhongshu (董仲舒, 179BC–104BC), who puts forward the idea of "human and Heaven respond to each other" (tian ren ganying, 天人感应). He has inherited his predecessors' thinking and believes that things of a similar nature could respond to each other:

> There are cloudy days, and there are sunny days. Similarly, a person can be in high spirits or become crestfallen. When a miasma arises in Nature, people, influenced by such an unhealthy air, will also have sadness growing inside him. For the same reason, when people are overcome by grief, a miasma, triggered by such grief, will rise in Nature. (Dong, 2015: 68)

It means that changes in nature affect human beings and their activities. At the same time, human actions and words, as well as the order or disorder of human society are also reflected in nature by astronomical signs. If the ruler of a state has said or done something treacherous, calamity or unnatural phenomenon of nature sometimes occur as a response. Dong Zhongshu, with this theory as his basis, tries to persuade the ruler to govern virtuously by citing historical calamities or unnatural phenomena.

Heaven still is the highest force and reacts towards human's behaviors, and human conducts activities following Heaven's orders. Heaven and human are no longer to be separated from each other but integrated to pursue the unity of them, just like Dong says, "Things are in the name of fame, fame is in the name of Heaven. Heaven and human beings are communicative; it is integrated into a whole" (Dong, 2001: 367). The Confucian "unity between Heaven and human" of Dong Zhongshu is developed a little from the previous generations. Heaven is still the supreme, but a human has the ability to correspond with Heaven in Dong's definition.

The Song Dynasty and the Ming Dynasty are the peaks of the development of Confucianism. During this period, "unity of Heaven and human" explores the relationship between Heaven and human from the internal world of human. The reason for exploring human's inner nature is that society is chaotic and turbulent during the Song and Ming Dynasties. Scholars could not realize their political ambitions. They turn their attention to the inner nature of human beings, which greatly develops the Confucian "unity of Heaven and human".

It is Confucian scholar Zhang Zai (张载, 1020-1077) in the Song Dynasty, who puts forward the complete concept of "unity of Heaven and human" for the first time. He regards *qi* (气, vital force) as the foundation of his theory to expound on the relationship of human and Heaven. *Qi* has a material existence independent of subjective consciousness, and it is the basic element of all physical beings. It is also the basis for the birth and existence of life and spirit. *Qi* is in a state of constantly moving and changing without any fixed shape. Its concentration gives birth to a thing and its evaporation symbolizes the end of that thing. It permeates all physical beings and their surroundings. All natural things, including living things and non-living things are originated from the one origin-*qi*. Human beings and natural things are formed existences by the vital force of Heaven and earth. That is why Confucian scholars think all the things in the world are similar regardless of their forms. Zhang Zai continues to explain as follows:

> A Confucian scholar is sincere because of his understanding, and he achieves understanding because of his sincerity. That is why Heaven and human are united as one, becoming a sage through studies, and master Heaven's law without losing comprehension of Human's law. (Zhang, 2009: 67)

It is the same as the idea that a true gentleman has ample virtue and cares for all things. This notion is an important part of the School of Principle in the Song and Ming Dynasties.

In the same period, Cheng Hao (程颢, 1032–1085) and his brother Cheng Yi (程颐, 1033–1107) are the core scholars of the Cheng-Zhu School of Confucianism in the 11th century. Cheng Hao is said to be the first to apprehend and revive Mencius's teachings in the Song Dynasty. Cheng Yi makes that claim for his brother shortly after Cheng Hao died:

> After the demise of the Duke of Zhou, the Way of the sages was not carried on, and after the death of Mencius, the teaching of the sages was not transmitted. When the Way was not carried on there was no good government for a hundred generations, and when the teaching was not transmitted, there were not true scholars for a thousand years. Even without good government, scholars could explain the way of good government for the edification of men and transmission to later generations, but without true [Confucian] scholars the world fell into darkness and people lost their way, human desires ran

amok, and heavenly principles were extinguished. The Master [Cheng Hao] was born 1, 400 years after Mencius and was able to recover the untransmitted teachings that survived in the classics, resolving to enlighten the people with the Way. (Cheng, 1981: 3–4)

Cheng Hao puts forward the concept of "natural law" (*tianli*, 天理), which is the essence of Heaven and the realm of ultimate significance. The term "natural law" means the universal law observed by all things in Heaven and on earth as well as by human society. "Everything except for manifestations of the natural law." (Cheng, 1981: 24) Natural law is the essence of the source of things, deciding the inherent nature of humans and things. In terms of human nature, natural law expresses itself in the innate good nature one is bestowed upon by heaven, as opposed to human desire. Cheng Hao divides human nature into "character endowed by *qi*" (*qizhi zhi xing*, 气质之性) and "character endowed by Heaven" (*tianming zhi xing*, 天命之性), and the two terms stand in contrast with each other. The term "character endowed by *qi*" encompasses two meanings. The first meaning refers to the specific disposition of a person under the influence of *qi*, such as firmness and gentleness, patience and impatience, and wisdom and stupidity. Biased and unkind behaviors of people originate from the "properties of *qi*". In this sense, the "properties of *qi*" and the "properties of Heaven and earth" together constitute a person's inborn character. The second meaning is that heavenly laws and *qi* influence a person's character together. As heavenly laws are embedded in the physical human body, they are influenced by *qi*. The interaction of moral characters endowed by heavenly laws and human desires reflect the properties of *qi* (vital force). In contrast, the "character endowed by Heaven" refers to the moral character endowed by Heaven to a person, also known as the "properties of Heaven and earth". "Characters endowed by Heaven" are purely good, providing the inner basis for a person's moral principle and conduct. However, as human characters are subject to other influences, "characters endowed by Heaven" can be obscured. Cheng Hao also says that "human being forms one body with Heaven and Earth and the Myriad Things", showing the unity of Heaven and man.

Zhu Xi (朱熹,1130–1200), a famous Confucian scholar in the Song Dynasty, proposes that "universal principle" (*li,* 理) exists in different things and manifests itself in different forms. "There is but one *li*, which exists in diverse forms." This is an important way in which the thinkers of the Song and Ming Dynasties view the existing forms of *li*. As *li* has different meanings, its one-and-diverse composition is also interpreted in different ways. One is as the origin of the universe in an ontological sense, *li* runs through all things. The *li* of each thing is not a part of *li*; it is endowed with the full meaning of *li*. Another is that universal *li* represents the universal law governing all things, and expresses itself in the form of different guiding principles in specific things. The *li* of each thing or being is a concrete expression of the universal *li*. As Zhu Xi (1986: 57) states, "*Li* (universal principle) runs through all things, which is derived from one source. But as *li* is present in different things, its functions and forms vary." The concept of *li* is one and ensures the unity of the world, whereas its diversity provides the basis for multifarious things and hierarchical order. Zhu Xi's concept of Heaven and tradition is central to the philosophic framework of Confucian thought and practice. Heaven (*tian,* 天) provides an absolute point of synchronic orientation that legitimizes the system by anchoring its values in the natural world. His concept of the Confucian tradition—the "succession of the Way" (*daotong,* 道统)—functions as a diachronic anchorage in the continuous "outflowing" (*liuxing,* 流行) of the "natural law of Heaven" (*tianli,* 天理), or the natural ordering process. Zhu Xi says that the universe is organic with life, in which human and nature are part of it. And all of them are united and governed by the natural law of Heaven in an interlinked way.

Wang Yangming (王阳明, 1472–1529), who is a Neo-Confucian scholar of the Song Dynasty, focuses not only on human nature but also on human heart/mind. "We have the identification of the heart/mind with Heaven and the Way,

The heart/mind is nothing but the Way, and the Way is nothing but Heaven." (Wang, 1993: 27) Hence the heart/mind is identical with the (Heavenly) principle. He believes that innate knowledge of human mind and principles of the universe are in liaison. It transcends time and space, and mind and *Dao* are universal for all mankind. All human beings, past and present, East or West, have a common innate knowing of truth and morality, and this is the basis for the common human identity. As Western and Chinese cultures come into contact increasingly after the Ming and Qing Dynasties, even though East and West differed in their academic cultures and much of the new knowledge differed in form from Chinese epistemology, their fundamental thinking could be reconciled. Wang Yangming holds that laws and nature are not two different things. To explore the laws of things means to find out their nature. Only through understanding and improving the world and human self can the harmony between humanity and all things be accomplished. His theory perfects the thought of "unity of Heaven and human". The Neo-Confucian scholars of the Song Dynasty develop the classical Confucianism thought of "the benevolent person loves others" and the thought of "extensive love to benefit all". It extends the scope of love to Heaven and earth and nature, and finally, achieves the ethical integration of Heaven and human.

In the Ming and Qing Dynasties, the Confucian concept of "unity of Heaven and human" is further expounded by Confucian scholar Dai Zhen (戴震, 1724–1777). He puts forward the concept of "perpetual growth and change", which can be understood concerning the existence of all things. It is the interaction of *yin* and *yang* that drives the process of endless cycle of birth, rebirth, and change of Heaven, earth and all things. This process is a fundamental attribute of the universe and the source of ethical behavior. He believes that change is the essence of the Way of Heaven. Heaven follows this principle, and human morality is guided by this principle such as the concept of benevolence and wisdom. Change is the state of universal movement, development, and the state of human life's change and continuances. Benevolence is the general rule of the development of nature and human, as well as the highest criterion of human morality. Moreover, Dai Zhen believes that human nature and morality correspond to the order of nature, that is, therefore the life is benevolence, the order is propriety, the decision is righteousness, and the store is wisdom. He puts "providence" and "goodness" of human relations into the "unity between Heaven and human". The idea of Dai Zhen reconstructs the ethical ontology of Confucianism from the theoretical perspective. Human ethics equates to the natural laws of Heaven, which guide human's social behavior, including human conduct and attitude towards nature. "Unity of Heaven and human" has become the basic ethical criterion of Confucianism with close-knit relationship with human ethics and the nature of Heaven.

Confucian "unity of Heaven and human" has been developed and enriched by Confucius and other Confucian scholars into a complete ideological system gradually. From what has been examined above, we can see that their thoughts mainly revolve around the three entities of Heaven, earth, and human. It is dealing with the relationship between human and nature, human and society, human and self, just like the statement in *Book of Rites*:

> The ancients, who wished to promote illustrious virtue under heaven, first had to rule their states well. Wishing to govern their states well, they first had to manage their fiefdoms well. Wishing to manage their fiefdoms well, they first had to cultivate themselves.

The above statement shows that nature, human, society, and self are interrelated and coexisted. And the fundamental requirement of a human being is the responsibility and morality of humankind. With moral ethics and natural conscience, human extends benevolence and love from filial scope to other people and finally to all things in the universe. It is the way to achieve a harmonious relationship between Heaven and human. Confucianism believes that the realistic way to achieve the unity of Heaven and human is moral cultivation and moral practice.

Confucian "unity of Heaven and human" mainly discusses the relationship between Heaven and human. Philosophers have different views on how to understand it, and the main difference lies in the definition of Heaven. In ancient Chinese culture, Heaven can be interpreted as Heaven of will, Heaven of destiny and Heaven of virtue, etc. The basic meaning refers to the physical sky or the entirety of nature (not including human society). Confucius in *The Analects* said, "Has Heaven ever said anything? The four seasons run their cyclical course and all things grow vigorously. Has Heaven ever said anything?" Here, Heaven refers to nature including four-season operation and the growth of all things. Besides, other philosophers as Xunzi, Liu Yuxi (刘禹锡) and Zhang Taiyan (章太炎) all have a theory of Heaven, referring to nature or the laws of nature.

Ancient Chinese scholars believe that Heaven, human, and earth are three major components of the universe. Since human being is a part of the universe, they should obey the universal law, which is also the basis of human nature, society, and morality. "Unity of Heaven and human" first concerns the harmony between human and nature. In addition, relation between people in society is another indispensable aspect of this thought. Human beings are the fundamental elements of society, and it is essential for an individual to have authentic virtues and moralities to become a complete human being. The ultimate goal of Confucianism is to achieve the unity of body and mind. In ancient times, due to the extremely low level of social productivity and human understanding, human couldn't understand the ever-changing forces of nature. Nature is bestowed with feelings by human beings to express their will with natural phenomena. Since nature is the basis of human beings' existence, in the following part the author explores the relationship between human and nature, which is the first main idea of "unity of Heaven and human".

Confucian "unity of Heaven and human" emphasizes the integrated relationship between human and nature. It advocates that human beings are part of nature and depends on nature. The relationship between human and nature is opposite as well as unified. On the one hand, it believes that human beings should respect nature and follow natural laws. On the other hand, it emphasizes human's subjective initiatives of utilizing nature for their survival and development. The harmony between nature and human is an ideal pursued by Confucius and later Confucian scholars. It is an important value and content of Confucianism. Human should take natural laws as the criterion of their behaviors, just like Confucius states in *The Analects*, "Heaven is the only one, Emperor Yao is the one who acts follow the Heaven." Here, Heaven refers to nature and Yao stands for human beings. Confucius means that nature has its laws of operation and human beings should follow the laws of nature.

Confucianism emphasizes to sustain the reproduction of natural resources, just as Dai Sheng says, "If it is not a suitable season for logging and hunting, it is the lack of filial piety." (Dai, 2009: 314) Mencius, inheriting Confucius' thought of benevolence, says in *Mencius*, "The benevolent man love others the man of propriety shows respect to others." In addition, Dong Zhongshu in the Han Dynasty expanded "benevolence" to love birds, insects, and other natural creatures. He believed that human should protect nature, and cherish all living things in the universe. These thoughts of the sages reflect that nature and human beings are an indivisible organic unity. Human should love nature to achieve harmony with nature for their own development.

Apart from the material sustenance that nature guarantees human beings, nature also gives guidance to them at the moral and psychological level. "Unity of Heaven and human" believes that human obtains truth and essence of being a man from the natural world. It claims that human moral characters are observed and learned from the natural world. This observation of nature is a kind of humanistic thinking. Human beings learn moralities of "filial piety" (孝) and "conscience" (良知), "rites" (礼), "righteousness" (义), "benevolence" (仁), and "loyalty" (忠), etc., from nature. For example, the feeding-back of a crow is an act of filial piety; the lamb to feed on its knees is an act of rites; and the deer to call friends to graze is an act of loyalty. According to Confucianism, human beings detect and learn morality embodied in animal behaviors, plants, even mountains and rivers from the natural world. Take the earth for example, just like the earth, which is generous and peaceful, a man of virtue should have ample virtue and accommodate all things. It means that one should be broad-minded and care for other people and things as the generous and peaceful earth. The earth sustains all things in the world, allowing them to grow and develop with their own nature. Human beings with virtue model themselves like the earth, caring for all things and other people with open hearts and virtues. It is of essential importance for human beings to observe nature and gain psychological guidance and support from the natural world. On the contrary, if human beings are separated from nature, they would lose spiritual guidance of nature and fall into the dilemma of spiritual crisis. Human beings need to maintain a close and harmonious relationship with nature to construct a complete human identity with moral characters.

To establish a harmonious relationship between human and nature, human should conform to the laws of nature and make use of nature for human development. As to the utilization of natural resources, human should take sustainability of the natural world seriously. Besides, nature is the moral basis for human beings and human society, providing spiritual and psychological support and guidance for human growth. Maintaining a harmonious relationship with nature is essential to human development. This section has analyzed the relationship between human and nature and has argued that the necessity of harmony between them, and the following part will focus on the second main idea of "unity of Heaven and human"—the relationship between human and society.

Living in the world, human beings inevitably have contact with other people and involve in different kinds of relationships. Human beings have social attributes, and an individual's existence in society is determined by various social relations. People can get a correct understanding of themselves and society by dealing with relationships with other people appropriately. The most basic relation in life is familial relations with family members since birth. When growing up, people come into contact with various relationships, such as political, legal, and moral relations in society. Since an individual can't live isolated in society, he/she builds his/her own identity and value gradually in society through interaction with others. The existence and development of human are based on various social relationships with others. If a person is born without a human social environment, he can't have the essence of human beings even with a developed brain and sound body. He is not different from animals. For example, although the wolf child has a similar body structure and function to human beings, it is not a real person. He can't talk but howl like wolves, and his temperaments are similar to wolves. He only has animal nature, which is a natural attribute, but does not possess any social attributes. Human nature is the combination of natural and social attributes, so wolf children are not real human beings. Social relations are essential for human existence, and it is of great importance for an individual to keep a harmonious relationship with other people. It includes relations with family members, with other people in society, and with the community.

Confucianism emphasizes the concept that "blood is thicker than water". The relationship between family members is the most important and basic relationship of an individual. Human beings are borne with familial relationships since the time that they came into the world. Familial relations include the relation between parents and children, relation between husband and wife, relation between elder and younger brothers, etc. As to the relation between parents and children, "unity of Heaven and human" advocates "filial piety" as the basis of establishing a harmonious relationship between them. According to Confucianism, filial piety is children's obedience, respect, and love for parents. There are three layers of meaning of filial piety: (1) Children should take good care of their bodies given by parents, and keep it safe from injury and illness so as not to let parents worry.

(2) Children should not go against parents' teachings, guidance, and requirements; and should obey them even if it does not agree with what the children think. (3) Children should gain fame and become accomplished through moral integrity, to highlight their parents' teachings and guidance.

Apart from children's responsibility for parents, as the most influential people for children's growth and well-being, parents should conduct the role of raising and educating children as well. Family is the foremost place for children's moral training and serves as the bridge between children and society. As to the significance of education, Confucian scholars put forward the concept of "enlightening the ignorant and making them follow the right path" (*meng yi yangzheng*, 蒙以养正). It means the ignorant should be enlightened through education so that they follow the right path. This education must begin from early childhood when parents act as the first teacher to children's growth. *Meng* (蒙) here refers to the naivety of the young and their lack of knowledge. *Yang* (养) means education. *Zheng* (正) suggests the right path, the proper way, and upright conduct. This term, which underlines Chinese pedagogy, and stresses the important function and value of education, including education of parents. Parents are expected not only to provide material needs for children but also to take responsibility for raising their children in morally sound environment. Parents are also required to make a harmonious environment for children's growth. In Confucianism, the environment in which children are growing up plays a vital role in their moral cultivation.

Except for the relationship between parents and children, the relationship between elder and younger brothers is also important in family. In Confucianism, this relationship is named "fraternal duty" (*ti*, 悌), which means love and respect for elder brother. The younger brother must follow an elder brother's guidance and orders. Fraternal duty should be rooted in heartfelt love and respect for an elder brother. Confucius often speaks of "fraternal duty" and "filial piety" together, believing that they are the foundation for cultivating personal moral integrity. And they are the basis for maintaining and strengthening family ethics, extending even to the political order. As one of Confucius's disciple, Youzi says in *The Analects*:

> It is rare for a person who is filial to his parents and respectful to his elders to be inclined to transgress against his superiors. And it has never happened that a person who is not inclined to transgress against his superiors is inclined to create chaos. A gentleman looks after the roots. With the roots firmly established, a moral way will grow. Is it not true then that being filial to one's parents and being respectful to one's elders is the root of one's humanity?

Fraternal duty and filial piety are the two most important relationships in familial scope as Youzi says, which are the basis of developing other ethics of an authentic human being. Being a good family member reverberates through society. A person who is good to their parents and siblings and children will be good to others as well. Self-transformation and benevolence begin in the family and spread outward. If an individual wants to grow into a person with a sound personality, he needs to establish a harmonious relationship with his parents as well as elder brothers in the family.

No one can live isolated in society, and people need to be accepted by society to establish his subjectivity. The premise of establishing self-identity is to deal with different relationships with other people. Confucianism advocates that "benevolence" (*ren*, 仁) is the highest moral principle. It is also the moral standard people should apply when interacting with other people in society. The basic meaning of benevolence is the love for others. Its extended meaning refers to the unity of all things under Heaven. It has the implications of compassion or conscience to other people and creatures in the universe. Confucius puts forward the concept in *The Analects* that "Do not impose on others what you do not desire for yourself". As a benevolent person, one should consider things from perspective of others and respect others' thoughts. For Confucius, a person earns respect from others by respecting other people. It centers on that a person should be considerate and extend his considerations to the wants and needs of others.

The relationship between an individual and community is also one aspect of human-society relationships in Confucianism. The harmony of individual and community lies in the fact that the two are interdependent and jointly promote each other's development. Just like only one note can't make perfect music, diversity of individuals in community can better promote the development of the community. And in turn community creates a stable environment for the growth of individuals. Diversity is the precondition of generating harmony in community. Moreover, an individual also needs to hold a communitarian notion of self. It means an individual should realize that he is a member of the community and should be responsible for it. Confucianism holds the view that if a person lives without communitarian notion, his actions result in excessive individualism which "not only endangers the well-being of others but also is detrimental to our own wholesomeness" (Tu, 1998: 305). The communitarian notion of being a person asks an individual to love and care for others to construct a reliable community. The harmony of an individual and community is achieved on their interdependent relations.

Everyone interacts with other people in society. Clear social norms and value standards should be established, and people should know their position and responsibility in society. To achieve universal harmony in society, people of different races, cultures, and gender should bear the morality of benevolence toward other people. In Confucianism, an individual needs to extend his love for parents and brothers to other people in society, and finally construct a harmonious society. And it is through the harmonious construction of relations with family members, with others in society, and with community that a person establishes his self-identity as an authentic human being. Having defined the relationship between human and society, this book moves on to discuss the third main idea of "unity of

Heaven and human"—the relationship between human and self.

Human is the only creature with subjective initiative that is different from animals and plants in the universe. Human needs to learn to live in harmony with the inner self, which is the highest goal pursued by Confucian scholars for thousands of years. Human beings have spiritual and physical composite and need to handle the relationship between spirit and body. The way to deal with the relation between them is to restrain desires and manage behaviors in society. In Confucianism, there are lots of descriptions about how to reach harmony with the inner self. "Unity of Heaven and human" emphasizes respecting oneself and self-discipline. The most fundamental way is to improve one's moral character and cultivate one's personality, which is essential for becoming a sage with a united body and mind. Among the moral characters, there are concepts like "benevolence" (*ren*, 仁), "righteousness" (*yi*, 义), "rites" (*li*, 礼), "wisdom", (*zhi*, 智), "good faith" (*xin*, 信), "considerate" (*shu*, 恕), "sincerity" (*cheng*, 诚), "restraining desires" (*guayu*, 寡 欲) and so on. With these moral characters and virtues, a person can successfully control his words and deeds as well as restrain his desires in life. These moralities can be interpreted as the qualities required for a person to cultivate personalities and become an authentic person.

Confucian "unity of Heaven and human" emphasizes that moral cultivation and practice are the logical cornerstones for achieving the harmonious relationship between human and the inner self. Xunzi believes that human beings are the noblest creature in the universe because of their moral characters:

> Fire and water possess a spirit but no life, grass and trees possess a life but no awareness, birds and animals possess awareness but no sense of morality, only human beings possess spirit, life, awareness, as well as the sense of morality, hence the noblest beings in the world. (Wang, 1978: 126)

The above words show that morality is the reason why human beings are nobler than other creatures. And the cultivation of one's personality and morality is an important way to achieve harmony with the inner self.

In Confucianism, a sage would sacrifice everything to maintain his virtues to become an exemplary person with a harmonious relationship with his inner self. "The determined scholar and the man of virtue will not seek to live at the expense of injuring their virtue. They will even sacrifice their lives to preserve their virtue complete." (*Mencius*, 1992: 206) Mencius also advocates that "Life is my desire, and righteousness is also my desire. But if I cannot get both together, I would rather choose righteousness than life" (*Mencius*, 1992: 482). People with a complete inner self know their value of life clearly and pay everything even death to stick to the values which eventually lead to the completion of their body and mind. On the contrary, a person without moral characters and virtues inevitably conduct some behaviors, which influences the well-being of others as well as his own. To reach the harmony between man and the inner self, people need to cultivate morality because this is the guiding principle of his thinking and behavior. And it takes a long time, just as the words stated by Confucius, "Cultivating one's heart-mind is almost a life-long journey." The goal of attaining self-discipline, self-mastery, or self-perfection takes a lifetime.

Now it has become more important to review and learn from ancient wisdom. Today's society, dominated by science, gives priority to science and technology development. And relatively little attention is given to human ethics and morals. Confucian teachings within this context play an important role in maintaining a better balance between technology and the spiritual world. Confucius' teachings, such as self-cultivation, moral characters, and family harmony help to acquire a better balance between "material progress" and "spiritual progress". "Unity of Heaven and human" pursues not only the harmony between human and the outside world but also the harmony between human and the inner life. It is a collective thought dealing with the relationship between human and nature, human and society, and human with the inner self. These thoughts guide human to understand the meaning and value of life. As the core of Chinese traditional values, it is a precious traditional culture to promote the social development of China as well as other countries in the world.

All human beings, past and present, East or West, have a common innate knowledge of truth and morality. While the "unity of Heaven and human" is developed in China, it has a certain influence on Western culture as well. From Morrison's connection with China and other Western philosophers that were influenced by Confucianism, we draw the conclusion that she is influenced by Confucianism on her thoughts and writing. To examine and prove the Confucian influence on Morrison's works is the purpose of this study. This book is consisted of the following structure.

1.5 Outline of the Book

The book tries to study Morrison's works with Confucian "unity of Heaven and human". There are various characters can be adopted as subjects to study from Morrison's eleven novels. In this book, only some of the characters are selected for discussion. This section turns to the outline of this book.

This book is composed of five chapters. The first chapter is the introductory part, which introduces the life and literary works of Toni Morrison, present study on Morrison and her works, research significance and methods, introduction of the Confucian "unity of Heaven and human", and outline of this book. Morrison's literary career can be divided into three stages according to her writing content. In this section, the author briefly introduces the content of each novel and writing characteristics of Morrison. In literature review part, various studies of her literary ideas and works have been introduced. Critics study her novels from perspectives of narrative strategies, female discourse, racial criticism, post-colonial criticism, psychological analysis, and so on. In Morrison's novels, some of her characters are faced with different kinds of predicaments and lack of self-identity. Morrison also depicts some characters with complete self-identity and independent personality. Having explained the connection between Morrison and Confucianism above, the author tries to study her novels with Confucian thought of "unity of Heaven and human". The main ideas of "unity of Heaven and human" revolve around human relationship with nature, with other people, and with the inner self. The author carries out the discussion according to the three main ideas of "unity of Heaven and human". Until now, there has not been any research of Morrison's connection to Confucianism. This book would broaden the study of Morrison to a certain extent.

The main body of this book is from Chapter 2 to Chapter 4. These three chapters study Morrison's works with three main ideas of "unity of Heaven and human" accordingly. Chapter 2 focuses on exploring the relationship between human and nature in Morrison's novels. "Unity of Heaven and human" advocates the mutual respect and harmonious relationship between human and nature. It holds the view that nature not only provides material products for human beings but also provides spiritual strength and support for their survival. In Morrison's works, nature also occupies an important position. There are plenty of descriptions of harmonious and disharmonious relationships between human and nature in her novels. The author adopts some typical examples to demonstrate human relationship with nature. In this part, characters in *Song of Solomon*, *Tar Baby*, *Love*, *Paradise*, *and A Mercy* are selected as the subjects to demonstrate human destruction and domination of nature, and alienation from nature. Their behaviors lead to physical and psychological destruction to human self. On the contrary, other characters who keep a close and harmonious relationship with nature live a self-reliant life and gain spiritual support from nature. Similar to the thought of "unity of Heaven and human", Morrison depicts human's relations with nature with two different kinds of characters to show the necessity of keeping a close and harmonious relationship with nature for human's benefit.

Chapter 3 focuses on the relationship between human and society in Morrison's works. Industrialization exerts a negative influence on relationship between human beings. As a humanist writer who is concerns about the living conditions and spiritual world of human beings, Morrison tries to explore ways to construct harmonious relationships among people. She attaches great importance to social relations in human life, including interpersonal link between family members and with others in society. In her novels, characters suffer from psychological trauma and loss of self-identity because of their distorted familial and social relations. Morrison emphasizes the importance of keeping a close relationship with family members and other people in society. "Unity of Heaven and human" also regards familial relationship as the most important one for an individual. It advocates children's filial piety to parents and parents' love for children. Moreover, it emphasizes the importance of constructing relationships with other people in society for an individual's growth. In this part, the author adopts the counter-argument to prove the idea of "unity of Heaven and human" reflected in Morrison's works. The author selects some characters from *The Bluest Eye*, *Sula*, *Song of Solomon*, *Beloved*, *Home*, *Paradise*, and *God Help the Child* as subjects to demonstrate the necessity of keeping harmonious relations with family members and other people in society.

Chapter 4 concentrates on the relationship between human and the inner self in Morrison's novels. To achieve the harmony of body and mind is the ultimate goal of Confucianism. It believes that human needs to have morality and virtue as well as sense of self-love and self-value to construct self-identity as a complete human being. Morrison depicts many characters with a high moral standard and an independent self-identity in her novels. At the same time, some characters are spiritual barrenness because of their lack of morality and self-love. In *The Bluest Eye*, *Sula*, *Tar Baby*, *Paradise*, *A Mercy*, characters that are lack morality and virtue and self-love fail to construct their self-identity. Whereas, some characters in *Love*, *Paradise*, and *God Help the Child* achieve harmony with their inner self with morality and self-love. Both "unity of Heaven and human" and Morrison advocate the necessity of possessing morality and virtue as well as self-love and self-value for human to achieve the highest pursuit of harmony with the inner self.

Chapter 5 is the conclusion part that summarizes our understanding of Morrison's works with Confucian "unity of Heaven and human". This book proves that Confucianism has influenced Morrison's writing to some extent. Moreover, this book holds the view that it is not an easy thing to establish and maintain a harmonious, peaceful relationship between human and nature, human and society, human and self. How to carry on the cultural and social functions of Confucian "unity of Heaven and human" in the world of fury remains a problem deserving of our exploration and efforts in the future. So far in this chapter, the author has studied the previous research on Morrison and three key aspects of Confucian "unity of Heaven and human". The following chapter attempts to read Morrison's novels from the relationship between human and nature.

2

Relationship Between Human and Nature

Confucian "unity of Heaven and human" consists of three categories of relationships, including the relationship between human and nature, human and society, and human and the inner self. Since nature is the basis of human existence and provides spiritual support for human, this chapter moves on to discuss the relationship between human and nature reflected in Morrison's novels. As the author examined in the introduction, the term Heaven has a lot of meanings. In this book, the author uses the term of Heaven to mean three things, that is, physical nature, spiritual being and universal laws. Confucius sometimes uses Heaven as a synonym for Fate or for Nature. Heaven is employed to stand for nature at large and for the energy and activity displayed by a power other than that from human. It indicates the great and invisible power of nature. Confucians have many ways of looking on nature. "They were interested in natural phenomena and human nature, and wandered about the relationship of human beings to the broader world around them." (Graham, 1989: 241) In this book, the meaning of nature refers to the physical nature. Confucianism respects nature as a divinity and believes that it is a power working for righteousness in the universe. Nature is regarded as the medium between Heaven and human, and human can obtain revelation from nature by different natural phenomena.

"Unity of Heaven and human" holds the view that human and nature are interdependent and inseparable in the universe. Confucian scholar Zhang Zai describes their relationship as follows:

Heaven is my father and Earth is my mother and even such a small creature as I find an intimate place in their midst. Therefore, that which fills the universe I regard as my body and that which directs the universe I consider as my nature. All people are my brothers and sisters, and all things are my companions. (Zhang, 2009: 58)

He believes that human and nature are closely connected, and everything existing in nature should love and respect each other. His thought transcends the old anthropocentric viewpoint and aims to reach a harmony between human and other creatures in nature. The relationship between human and nature is based on reciprocal respect for one another. Human beings rely on nature to provide them with food, water, shelter, and other living necessities. And they utilize natural materials and energy to develop human society. Human also should respect and protect nature, and conform to natural laws. The reason we give our affection to nature is that it provides spiritual consolation and support as well as moral cultivation for human. Zhang Zai thinks that humanity is providence and believes that "humanity and providence are easy to just change" (Zhang, 2009: 60), which means that human can practice beyond their limitations and reach the infinite virtue of Heaven. In summary, nature not only provides material resources with which human can survive but also spiritual support for human beings. "Unity of Heaven and human" advocates the mutual-respect and harmonious connection between human and nature. There is a phrase in Confucianism, "No one is saved until we are all saved", here the "one" includes not only human beings, but all creatures, animals, forests, mountains and rivers, tiniest microbes in the universe. The existence and development of all things, including human beings, is wholly organic and influenced by each other in nature. Since human beings are a part of the natural world and interrelated with nature, harming nature is harming humans themselves.

Morrison cherishes the same love and appreciation for the natural world. Nature occupies an important position and is an indispensable element for her story construction. She is especially sensitive to the perception of nature in her works. Barbara Christian states in "Community and Nature: The Novels of Toni Morrison" as follows:

> [t]he interpretation of Nature is not only central to her characters' attempts to understand themselves but to the fables Morrison weaves, the way she tells her tales. The return to black culture and the importance of nature are important themes in Morrison's novels. The understanding of nature not only enables people to know themselves but also facilitates Morrison to narrate plots. Toni Morrison endows nature in her novels with so important a significance that few persons, among the contemporary American novelists, do like her on that. (Christian, 1980: 75)

In this essay, Christian argues that the interpretation of nature is not only an important theme in Morrison's novels but also one of the major structural elements of their composition. Furthermore, numerous vivid descriptions of natural scenery are depicted in Morrison's novels. Through describing the destruction of rivers and plants and animals, Morrison shows the ruthless exploitation and plunders of nature by human beings. As nature is the basis of human existence as well as sources for human maintenance, Morrison criticizes human beings' domination and exploitation of nature in her novels. Morrison points out that human and nature ought to keep an intimate relation with each other. As far back as human society developed, man and nature were originally in perfect harmony and interdependent with each other:

> What the exchange between man and nature depends upon is not the language, but signs existing long before the formation of languages and appearing of writing. However, it can also be deemed to be a language, a language of the times that man and animals talk indeed with each other, a person and an ape can sit together intimately, a man will share a tree with a

tiger and they understand each other well, and people run in company with wolves instead of escaping or chasing them. And mankind may hear such a language in the mountains, under a eucalyptus sending forth a delicate fragrance. If a man can converse with nature and nature with man, what, then, cannot be understood between them? (Warren, 1996: 24)

Morrison insists that human and nature can understand each other and keep a harmonious relationship with each other. In her works, Morrison not only gives vivid descriptions of natural scenery but also displays the generous rendering of nature to human in both substance and spiritual world. She expresses her keen interest and deep gratefulness to nature. In her view, nature is not only the spatial environment in which human lives but also their sacred spiritual home. Human should love nature, blend into nature, and seek the tranquility of the inner world under the care and influence of nature.

Due to her African American identity, Morrison pays more attention to the fate and destiny of the black race and culture as well as African Americans' identity construction. The main characters in her novels are African Americans. Nature plays a sacred role in African culture and people worship nature with great awe. Edward Blyden also points out that black people's close communion with nature is a special trait of the black race, as he said, "[T]he African ... is to pursue the calling of man when in his perfect state ... His real work ... is to speak to the earth and let it teach him." (Blyden, 1964:78) However, due to industrialization, numerous African Americans moved from the rural south to the urban north, from the southern nurturing family and friends to the isolation and alienation of northern cities. As a result, their belief in nature has been changed radically. Among Morrison's works, there are many descriptions of human attitudes and behaviors toward nature. Some of her characters fail to realize the significant role of nature to human and destroy nature mercilessly, which leads to their self-destruction. Whereas, those people who keep an intimate relationship with nature meet not only their material needs but also gain spiritual support from nature. This chapter examines Morrison's novels from both the harmonious and disharmonious relationships between human and nature, so as to provide evidence for Morrison's demonstration of the Confucian "unity of Heaven and human" in her writing. In the following section, the author deals with the disharmonious relationship between human and nature and goes on to discuss the harmonious relationship.

2.1 Disharmonious Relationship Between Human and Nature

In the early stage of human society, human beings and nature are connected together by original agricultural production and plantation. Human not only gets material needs from nature to survive but also attains inner peace and spiritual purification in nature. However, rapid industrialization in the twentieth century brought about a radical change to human, life and drove them to pursue material accumulation by exploiting natural resources excessively. Human transforms nature for profits regardless of sustainability of the natural world. Human behaviors destroy the originally harmonious relationship between human and nature. In her works, Morrison describes human beings' violent destruction and exploitation of nature that lead them to self-destruction at last. Just as the sayings of Confucius that "Man who accords with Heaven can be preserved, Man who rebels against Heaven can perish" (Annping, 2014: 134). Apart from the destruction and domination of nature, human alienation from nature is also described by Morrison in her novels.

2.1.1 Destruction and Domination of Nature

Abundant natural images occurred In Morrison's novels, such as wilderness, forests, mountains, rivers, and trees, etc. Morrison shows humans ' ruthless exploitation and destruction of nature through these entities. As explained in the previous chapter, Morrison is concerned more about the fate and development of the whole humankind in the third stage of her writing career. Since nature plays an important role in human development, Morrison spends a lot of space describing the relationship between human and nature in her novels, especially in *Paradise*, *Love,* and *A Mercy*. In the following part, the book examines human's destructive activities towards nature in these three novels.

In *Paradise*, the original model of farm plantation, which used to connect black people with nature closely, tends to decline in the developed northern area. The booming growth of the population after industrialization and unwise strategy of land utilization destroy the relations between human and nature. People in Ruby Town become wealthy and self-sufficient by selling lands to various companies. They possess the same technological products as white people, "In every Ruby household appliances pumped, hummed, sucked, purred, whispered and flowed" (*Paradise*, 89). These well-designed household appliances, fancy clothes, and luxurious cars which only belong to whites in the past, now also appear in African Americans' daily life. They take these products as trophies from industrialization. They destroy and sell the farmland they used to plow and race their horses when they first settled here. People in Ruby are overwhelmed by the commercial culture which directs them in the wrong direction of life. Steward Morgan, the richest person who once owned a farm, takes control of Ruby Town. Afterward, he sells it to a gas company for money, "in 1962 the natural gas drilled to ten thousand feet on the ranch filled his pockets but shrunk their land to a toy ranch, and they lost the trees that had made it so beautiful to hold" (82). He takes the land as property which can be used to make profits. Western culture believes that human can dominate nature, conquer nature, and transform nature according to human will. This concept is likely to lead to anthropocentrism and the omnipotence of science and technology. Science and technology has become the priority of human consideration. Human beings loss their subjectivity gradually and eventually led to their self-destruction.

Unlike other novels written by Morrison, there is little natural scenery depicted in *Paradise*. Instead, Morrison's awareness of nature has been revealed vividly by describing people's greedy exploitation of natural resources under the guise of modern industrialization. The appeal to return to nature is an important theme in *Paradise*. As a writer concerned about nature conservation and sustainable development, Morrison shows in *Paradise* that human beings are the direct destroyer and exploiter of natural resources. Morrison also describes nature's destructive revenge to human in the novel. Because of industrialization, the original harmonious connection with nature has been overshadowed by the desire for money. The invisible bond between nature and human has gradually disappeared, which causes the survival crisis of human beings.

Unlike the Western ideas of "Man can conquer nature", the "unity of Heaven and human" views the relationship between human and nature within the scope of the whole universe and integrates the two into one. Confucianism believes that human beings ought to coexist with nature and should not transform nature without limit. In fact, different from the Western concern with the external value of things, Confucianism is concerned with the intrinsic value of things. As scholar Qiao Qingju argues:

> The nobility of human nature in Confucianism is not about "conquering and controlling nature" but "showing itself in its ability to recognize and follow the way of nature, assisting it in its own completion". (Qiao, 2013: 27–28)

Confucianism goes further to demand that everything realizes its nature to bring into full play its natural endowment, instead of squandering what is endowed by Heaven, with a marked acknowledgment of the intrinsic value of everything. And in this respect, the Confucian doctrine of "unity of Heaven and human" surpasses Western anthropocentrism.

Anthropocentrism believes that human beings are the dominator of the universe and have the right to make use of natural world according to their particular need. Nature crisis is caused by human's unlimited exploitation of natural resources with the development of modern civilization. This is evidently described in Morrison's eighth novel, *Love*. People don't have the consciousness of protecting nature but destroy it without mercy.

In this novel, with the development of technology, the relationship between human and nature becomes more and more tense. Human exploits productive resources from nature, but pays little attention to environmental protection. The trace of human activities can be seen everywhere in the natural world. Primitive forests are transformed into cities, rivers are polluted by factories, and land is destroyed by human society. Human beings destroy nature mercilessly to gain material accumulation. The story takes place in an eastern coast town called Silk, where Bill Cosey lives a rich and superior life with his hotel business. Cosey Hotel is built in a coast country and the scenery is beautiful. It has become the best-known vacation spot on the eastern coast. The beautiful natural scenery and cozy climate provide people with a wonderful place to enjoy themselves:

> Our weather is soft, mostly, with a peculiar light. Pale mornings fade into white noons; then by three o'clock, the colors are savage enough to scare you. Jade and sapphire waves fight each other, kicking up enough foam to wash sheets in. An evening sky behaves as though it's from some other planet—one without rules, where the sun can be plum purple if it wants to and clouds can be red as poppies. Our shore is like sugar, which is what the Spaniards thought of when they first saw it. (*Love*, 7)

We can see that the natural scenery is awesome in Cosey Resort. It attracts tourists from the whole country, and the Cosey family becomes the most wealthy and prosperous on Up Beach. However, they do not cherish natural beauty at all. They build a cannery factory and the smell released by the factory ruins the fresh air. "Nobody could get enough of our weather except when the cannery smell got to the beach and into the hotel." (8) They focus only on industrial development regardless of the environmental protection. And their action has paid a heavy price. Nature starts to revenge on humankind through natural disasters. Though the Cosey family is prosperous, they can't do anything in front of natural power. Up Beach is hit by a hurricane named Agnes and goes through a drought:

> Hurricanes following droughts, marshland turned into mud cakes so dry even the mosquitoes quit; and people in Up Beach "pumped mud from their spigots". Dried-up wells and Brackey water scared them so. (9)

Cosey Hotel is also destroyed in this hurricane. Though it is still standing on Up Beach, "[It] looks more like it's rearing backward—away from the hurricane and a steady blow of sand" (107). The prosperity of the family in the past is gone forever. "Hills of sand piling in porch corners and between banister railings are whiter than the beach and smother, like twice-shifted flour. Fox-glove grows waist-high around the gazebo."(7) The beautiful natural environment of Cosey Hotel in Up Beach has deteriorated because of human's merciless exploitation and destruction. Just like Rousseau says that if the destruction to nature gets worse and worse, nature not only "swallows up the whole natural world in the end" but becomes "the cause making us carry on misdeeds, thus transforming us into slaves and keeping us in bondage by corrupting us" (Rousseau, 2010: 63).

What people have done to nature in this novel is a typical example of anthropocentrism. Unlike anthropocentrism, Confucian scholar Meng Peiyuan (蒙培元) holds the view that the fundamental difference between Confucianism and anthropocentrism is that the former is concerned with human value while the latter is concerned with profits. Meng explains the reason why human beings are the noblest creation of Heaven and earth. It is because they possess the ability to achieve harmony with nature:

> Human beings are the noblest because they realize their nature by accomplishing the heavenly mission and completing the way of production and reproduction in the natural world so that everything follows and enjoys its natural course of life. It is from the harmony between human and nature that human derives their greatest joy and happiness. (Meng, 2007: 10)

By depicting the scenery before and after the hurricane, Morrison attempts to show the importance of protecting nature and keeping a harmonious relationship with nature. And human needs to keep a balanced relationship with the natural world to avoid revenge from nature.

In *A Mercy,* Morrison depicts D'Ortega as a slave of his material desires. As a tobacco planter, he possesses vast farmland and numerous slaves. D'Ortega is never satisfied with what he has possessed, and he wants to earn more money through the slave trade. But something unexpected happens, "disaster had struck ... D'Ortega's ship had been anchored a nautical mile from shore for a month waiting for a vessel ... a third of his cargo had died of ship fever" (*Mercy*, 16). His dream of making more profits is dashed. To save money, he throws away those dead bodies near bay Adlib. The dead and rotten bodies pollute seawater, and the putrid odor of dead bodies also poisons the air. D'Ortega only cares about his profits and disposes of those bodies in a perfunctory way. Though D'Ortega is "fined five thousand pounds of tobacco by the Lord Proprietary' magistrate for throwing their bodies too close to the bay" (16), and ordered to clear up the bodies, he just orders his men to cast aside the bodies in a remote place. He gives a cold shoulder to the impact on the environment and people living in the neighborhood. The bay is near the port where many vessels come and go every day. What's more, a lot of residents live nearby, and their daily life is closely connected to the natural environment of the bay. Through D'Ortega's behavior, Morrison shows human's infinite desire for material wealth accumulation regardless of environmental protection. Morrison aims at telling people that the unrestrained material desire of human beings not only harms nature but also affects human beings themselves.

Confucius pays attention to restrain human's material desire in his teaching. He calls for the pursuit of material wealth on the premise of fulfilling the responsibility of protecting nature. As Confucius says, "Wealth and eminence are what people desire. If you cannot acquire them by proper means, you should not accept them." (Annping, 2014: 79) For Confucius, it is better to abandon the wealth if it is obtained in an inappropriate way. D' Ortega acquires his money by polluting the natural environment, which is opposed by both Confucianism and Morrison. They all advocate restraining material desire to protect nature.

In this novel, Lina tells Florens the story of an eagle. This story shows that human beings are superior to other creatures in the world. An eagle builds its nest on top of a mountain to protect the eggs from being eaten by snakes or birds; however, it can't keep its eggs away from the invasion of human beings:

> One day a traveler climbs a mountain nearby. He stands at its summit admiring all he sees below him. The turquoise lake, the eternal hemlocks, the starlings sailing into clouds cut by the rainbow, the traveler laughs at the beauty saying, "This is perfect. This is mine." And the word swells, booming like thunder into valleys, over acres of primrose and mallow ... Mine. Mine. Mine. The shells of the eagle's eggs quiver and one even cracks. The eagle ... swoops down to claw away his laugh and his unnatural sound. But the traveler ... raises his stick and strikes her wing with his strength. Screaming she falls and falls ... she is carried away by wind instead of the wing. (62)

This part reflects the desire of human beings to control other creatures, and human destruction of the natural world. They are not satisfied with owning land, houses and property, they want to control the whole world. They take all living things in nature as their own assets. The immoderate exploitation and destruction of nature ultimately destroys the harmony between nature and human. In her works, Morrison shows that other species on the earth are the same as human beings. "Yellow, and green birds, playful foxes or the rose-tinted clouds collecting at the edge of the sky are equally lovely." (80) As Lucretius says, "Nature consists of all things on earth, not just mankind." (Lucretius, 2004: 27) Confucianism perceives all natural beings as members of a moral community, and human should treat them equally and morally. In Confucian philosophy, "the scope of the moral community includes animals, plants, as well as objects of the inanimate world, such as stones and clay" (Qiao, 2011: 18). Benevolence is not applied solely to human society but to all things in the universe, just as the remark of Meng Peiyuan, "Confucius' deep respect, compassion, and concern for every form of life in nature" (Meng, 2007: 36).

Apart from these three novels, Morrison also describes the destruction and domination of human beings towards the natural world in other novels. Her first novel, *The Bluest Eye* is an example. Morrison describes the environmental pollution caused by industrialization, as the narrator of the story Claudia says:

> Later we walk home, glancing back to see the great carloads of slag being dumped, red hot and smoking, into the ravine that skirts the steel mill. The dying fire lights the sky with a dull orange glow. (*Bluest*, 22)

The smoke released from the steel mill pollutes the environment of human beings. In addition, at the beginning of *Sula*, Morrison depicts human's behaviors of changing natural land into towns and suburbs without protecting natural scenery. "In that place, where they tore the nightshade and blackberry patches from their roots to make room for the Medallion City Golf Course, there was once a neighborhood." (*Sula*, 14) It is evident that human destroys the natural land to meet their life needs unscrupulously.

Morrison describes vividly how human beings exploit and destroy the natural world regardless of natural protection. She believes that human and nature depend on each other. Human needs material and spiritual support from nature. Morrison hopes to make a world that human and nature can exist harmoniously. She believes that "the need for a new cosmology and new anthropology which recognizes that life in nature (which includes human beings) is maintained utilizing cooperation, and mutual care and love" (Mckay, 1983: 419). And Confucian "unity of Heaven and human" believes that human beings are not the conqueror and the occupant, but the protector of nature. Just as Ji Xianlin states, "unity of Heaven and human" is that "Man and nature are to be united, and be in peaceful coexistence, not to speak of conquest and subjugation" (Ji, 2011: 25). What is more important is that human beings should keep a harmonious and coexisting relationship with nature as Ji Xianlin say in the above citation. As described previously, human destruction and domination of the natural world has been described in *Paradise*, *Love*, and *A Mercy*. Another aspect of disharmonious relations between human and nature— human's alienation from nature, is examined in the following section.

2.1.2 Alienation from Nature

In Morrison's novels, because of the industrialization, some characters migrate from the south to the north. The migration leads to their alienation from nature. When living in the south, they have a close connection with nature and can gain spiritual support from nurturing family and friends. On the one hand, they are limited to agrarian activities on the plantation. They carry on farming, craft making, singing, and other activities in traditional African ways. They maintain a close connection with nature in the south, though with geographical difference from Africa. On the other hand, they are treated as the property of white people and forbidden to participate in any social and economic activities. They have to assemble together and maintain close connections with family members and people in the community. They obtain strength and courage from other people to face the discrimination and isolation from the white people. Edward Blyden says that one of the special characteristics of the African race is their close communion with nature. According to Blyden (1967: 48), "the close communion with nature enables Africans to establish social and cultural institutions best suited to their needs". In African culture, people help each other and distribute the product equally among the community members. They also keep a relatively low consumption of natural resources. It is in the south where the slaves first bring the African traditions with them. And their descendants have inherited and reshaped these traditions to establish their unique culture in America.

The north is "radically different from southern life" (Beavers, 1998: 64). In the north, nature seems to disappear in the lives of African Americans. With the development of industrialization in the north, people's attitudes toward nature have also been changed. Unlike southern ancestors who make a living out of the land, most of African Americans in the north have to work as factory workers or housemaids for white people. Gradually, they form a money-oriented value. After leaving the south, they have lost their connection with nature. Moreover, the black community becomes fragmented with each struggling for their survival. The changes from the agrarian rural south to the industrial urban north fundamentally changed the way of living and value systems of African Americans. As Bell Hooks pointed out, the "moving from the agrarian south to the industrialized north wounded the psyches of black folk" (Hooks, 1981: 29). Since they moved from the south to the north, they suffered great trauma in constructing their identities in American society. It is manifested in Morrison's novels, such as *Song of Solomon*, *Paradise*, and *A Mercy*.

Under the influence of industrialization, human beings' harmonious connection with nature has been overshadowed by their desire for money. Human beings are a part of the natural world, and they are bound to feel fear and anxiety when they are far away from nature. In *Song of Solomon,* Milkman's father, the second generation of Macon Dead, represents people who have lost their roots and culture while they seek wealth in the north. He leaves his hometown Montour County, Pennsylvania to the northern industrial city of Michigan. Macon is far away from the beautiful and attractive nature. Before Macon flees to the north, he enjoys the pastoral scenery and the care of the black community in the south. His childhood is close to nature, there are woods, a pond, and a stream full of fish near his home. Oaks, pines, and fruit trees are all around as well as hogs, deer, and wild turkey in the mountains. Macon recalls that the wild turkey his father cooks is the most delicious food in the world. "You ain't tasted nothing till you taste wild turkey the way Papa cooked it." (*Solomon*, 51) From birth to age sixteen, Macon lives in Lincoln's Heaven, the beautiful farm his father built from scratch in sixteen years. During that time, Macon is a hardworking and loyal boy. He works with his father on the farm and enjoys the delight of labor and the beauty of nature. It's the only period of time when his life is full of real happiness.

At that time, Macon is a good son, a loving brother, and an integral person. His sister Pilate is the most precious person for him in the world. Macon takes care of Pilate, just as she recalls, "Macon was a nice boy and awful good to me. Be nice if you could have known him then." (40) When Pilate is a baby, he carries her to another farm in his arms every morning and picks her back when he finishes working with his father. Macon often recalls the precious memory of Pilate making the cherry pie for him. But after he moves from the south to the northern industrial city, Macon becomes a businessman who is cold, selfish, and seldom smiles. He is ruthless and only cares about money. Only when he reminisces about the good old days to Milkman, Macon becomes soft and smiles, as "His voice sounded different to Milkman. Less hard, and his speech was different. More southern and comfortable and soft" (52). After witnessing the murder of his father by the white men's treachery and bullets, Macon "paid homage to his own father's life and death by loving what that father had loved— property, good solid property, the bountifulness of life" (300). His father's death makes him realize that he must take revenge by owning more properties. His view of property turns to "own it rather than living within it" (Christian, 1980:71). It means Macon's attitude of life is to accumulate wealth with the property. He will do anything at any price to obtain wealth and money.

Macon's money-oriented value is formed not only by industrialization but also because of his separation from nature. Moving to the north, he cares only about property and money without caring for other people in the community. Mrs. Bains is very poor and is a tenant of Macon Dead. She has two grandchildren to raise and no money to pay the rent for two months overdue. When she asks Macon for a delay of the rent, Macon declines with an ironical tone and only gives her deadline, "till Saturday coming, Saturday, Mrs. Bains. Not Sunday. Not Monday, Saturday" (21). Macon shows no mercy and sympathy to her at all, only wants to get his money. He has been assimilated by the values of industrialization completely, regarding wealth as the most important things in life above anything else.

Macon's ruthlessness towards other people makes him have a bad reputation in the community. Everyone doesn't like him. He is alienated from the black community and even his family members. Due to his lack of connection with nature, Macon's values have been distorted by the white money-oriented culture. He has alienated from nature after leaving his hometown in the south, and can't attain consolation and power from nature to become an integrated man with love and responsibility towards other people. Just as Lu Shuyuan says:

> Modern people's contempt for nature is consistent with the praise of artificial products, and their ignorance of natural beauty is consistent with the passion for white objects. It is the conflict between industrial civilization and nature, which leads to the disappearance of natural beauty from the human field of vision. (Lu, 2000: 84)

Morrison attaches great importance to nature in human's process of being a whole person in this novel just as Lu Shuyuan says in the above citation. If a man loses connection with nature, his value is distorted by industrial values. To become a complete person, human should get strength and consolation from nature by keeping a harmonious relationship with nature.

From the above mentioned, we can see that when Macon is in the south, he is a hardworking and upright person because of his close connection with nature and African traditions. After he moves from the south to the north, influenced by industrialization, he has turned into a snobbish, selfish, and materialistic businessman without mercy. Nature in the south stands for the root and spiritual home for African Americans. Being far away from nature, Macon feels psychologically alienated and fragmented in mind. He has become an irresponsible and ruthless person without a sense of belonging.

Another typical example is from Morrison's seventh novel, *Paradise*. People in Ruby Town are isolated from nature and gradually lose their responsibility of nature. Unlike their southern ancestors whose living depend on the land, most of African Americans immigrate to the industrialized northern areas. They begin to boast themselves and compete with each other for material collection. In the south, African Americans plant in the fields to meet their daily needs and share food with others in the community. In the north, everything has changed. For example, "The women kept on with their vegetable gardens in the back, but little by little its produce become like the flowers—driven by desire, not a necessity" (*Paradise*, 90). These gardens have become a property for these women to show off:

> As these gardens enable the Ruby women to compete with each other rather than to reproduce life to share and provision, they become another form of conspicuous consumption rather than necessary production. (Murphy, 2013: 220)

Gradually, they lose their gratitude towards their labor and nature. For

African American women, they are free from endless house chores and heavy labor work with the advanced machines. Women in Ruby plant for decoration, instead of daily needs. The beautiful scenery in Ruby is artificial without vitality. They have gone far away from the natural way of living. It is impossible for them to obtain real happiness from diligent labor and from the wild beauty in the natural world.

In a white-dominated society, African Americans have been discriminated against and isolated by white people from all aspects. They are assimilated by the standard of white beauty and want to be integrated into the white society. However, they are not allowed to enter into the white people's lives in America or go back to their original life in Africa. They have been deprived of the sense of belonging both in America and Africa. On the one hand, they are marginalized by white people in American society. On the other hand, they have lost the nourishment from African traditional culture and nature. As a result, their refusal to accept the traditional African value about nature and their failure to immerse in the white society lead to their absence and distortion of self-identity. Just as Kristin Hunt puts it:

> As the novel progresses, Morrison illustrates how this patriarchal mentality eventually fails to nurture a permanent bond between the townspeople and the land. Trying so desperately to pursue the American dream, the forefathers of the town set up boundaries between themselves, their wives and daughters, and the surrounding land ... But the founders of Ruby are determined to avoid any outside influences that may harm them, including those of nature itself. Ultimately, it is the refusal to accept nature's course and to form bonds with the environment that brings about the demise of the clan's descendants. (Hunt, 2000: 121–122)

Hunt holds the view that it is the alienated and disharmonious relationship with nature that leads to the self-destruction of the Ruby people.

At the very beginning of *Tar Baby*, Morrison depicts the island Isle des Chevaliers as the end of the world. It implies that this place has no future for human. Even clouds and fish are convinced that the world is doomed to be destroyed, "the sea-green of the sea and the sky-blue sky of the sky were no longer permanent" (*Tar Baby*, 7). Like the Eden garden, this quiet and beautiful place is doomed to be eliminated because of human's excessive material needs. When describing the changes of the natural world on the island, Morrison allows animals and plants to express their feelings towards what human beings have done to them. Morrison writes in *Rootedness* that:

> All of nature thinking and feeling and watching and responding to the action going on in *Tar Baby* so that they are in the story: the tree hurt, fish are afraid, clouds report, and the bees are alarmed. (Koener, 1984: 342)

Morrison adopts personification to show the destruction of nature by human beings, and to illustrate the disharmonious relationship between human and nature in this novel. Valerian Street, owner of the island, has trampled the land and cut down trees to build his house. His behavior has destroyed the sustainable use of land and the growth cycle of trees. Confucianism believes that natural resources are not inexhaustible. And human should abide by the laws of nature and have reverence for nature. Just like Confucius says, "The gentleman stands in awe of three things. He is in awe of Heaven's mandate, of great man, and the words of sages." (Annping, 2014: 319) That means human should have a sense of natural protection so that they can get rich living resources from nature. Otherwise, natural resources would be exhausted and eventually harm mankind itself. Regarding natural sustainable development, Confucian scholar Lv Buwei puts forward the concept of "ban on the four seasons":

In unsuitable seasons, it shall not cut down trees of the forest on the mountains, and not mow grasses and burn ashes in the water areas, capturing snares shall not be brought out of the door, fishing nets shall not be thrown into the water, and sailing boats shall not be made an excuse except for the officers in charge of the ships. Because of these things will hamper the farming season. (Lv, 2010: 334)

Confucianism advocates the conservation and reproduction of nature. Valerian does not care about natural protection and makes excessive use of natural resources to fulfill his needs. According to Philip Page (1999: 75), "the house that he has constructed is the symbol of Valerian's hegemony over nature". Valerian stands for the greedy people who overcome and change nature to satisfy their own desire, which leads to his alienated relationship with nature.

In nature, river is an important image. It supplies water for human beings, animals, and plants and affects the weather conditions. In this novel, Morrison describes that the river becomes a swamp, which causes the annihilation of the natural world on the island. As a result, the trees and wildflowers are destructed as the rain becomes very scarce:

[Then] the rain changed and was no longer equal. Now it rained not just for an hour every day at the same time, but in seasons, abusing the river even more. Poor insulted and broken-hearted river, poor demented stream... (20)

All these form a vicious circle that destroys the natural environment on the island that affects human life severely. The ecological cycle has been destroyed completely:

[The] wild parrots escaped from the island for another refuge, fish carries the news around the island; even the diamondbacks left the trees "for the new growth that came to life in spaces the sun saw for the first time". (21)

It is because the trees in the forest become less dense to block the sunshine. Other creatures in the natural world begin to resist human oppression with rebellion. In this novel, ants keep creeping into the house and plants in the greenhouse refuse to blossom. And the full moon beholds them at night and makes the white couple awakening the whole night. Even the champion daisy trees are planning for a war. Through description of the disordered nature, Morrison shows the conflicts between humankind and nature. In this sense, Isle des Chevaliers becomes a symbol of a virgin world which was revenged by nature due to human's own mistakes. As Pepsi said in "Talk with Toni Morrison" in *New York Times Book Review*:

> The world is alive: trees can be anger or sadness, and the birds are present or not present means a lot. You have to be vigil experience to that information; they also let you know your behavior.

Morrison believes that human should respect other creatures in nature, as they all have life and interrelated with human. In this section, it has been explored the disharmonious relationship between humans and nature in Morrison's novels. The following section moves on to examine the harmonious relationship between human and nature in Morrison's novels.

2.2 Harmonious Relationship Between Human and Nature

Confucianism holds the view that human and nature have the same essence and should maintain a harmonious relationship with each other. According to Dong Zhongshu in the Han Dynasty, human beings are a duplication of nature, naturally, they respond to each other. So he puts forward another theory, that is, "humanity should be aligned with nature". He believes that all things between Heaven and earth have their intrinsic structures and orders. Human's body, feelings, thinking, acts, and ethics are all in correspondence with the structure and order of nature, particularly in numbers:

> Human beings have 366 small joints, like the number of days of a year. We have 12 large joints, the number of months in a year. We have five organs, like the five elements. We have four limbs, like the number of seasons in a year. We open our eyes and close them the next, which is just like changes of day and night. We may be firm this moment and tender next, resembling winter and summer. We may become grieved this moment and joyful the next, like *yin* and *yang*. We have plans and concerns, which are patterned after the operation of Heaven and earth. We follow our ethics when acting, in compliance with the order of Heaven and earth. All these are inherent in us as soon as we are born. People and nature are matched in countable ways. In other aspects that cannot be expressed in numbers, our constitution corresponds with nature. Both countable and uncountable aspects conform to the laws of nature. (Dong, 2015: 154)

Human beings have the same structure as nature. Dong's idea provides the basis for mutual interaction and interdependence between human and nature. Moreover, as discussed in the introduction, Confucianism claims that human moral characters are learned from the natural world by observing the behaviors of animals. And nature is the moral basis for human beings, providing spiritual and psychological support and guidance for their growth. If human beings are separated from nature, they would lose the spiritual and moral guidance of nature and fall into the dilemma of spiritual crisis.

Morrison also pays great reverence to nature. In her opinion, human and nature should live in harmony among themselves. Human beings obtain inspiration and strength from nature and accept baptism of the soul. The interaction of nature and human greatly endows them with wisdom and power to survive on the earth. Both Confucianism and Morrison pay great reverence to nature and believe that nature is the spiritual home for human beings to obtain spiritual and moral support in life. In her works, Morrison depicts many characters that have a harmonious relationship with nature by respecting and maintaining a natural way of living, and some characters that gain spiritual and moral support from nature.

2.2.1 Natural Lifestyle

In Morrison's works, the representative figures of the black culture have a common characteristic. They keep a close connection with nature. For them, nature is equal to the traditional culture of the black race, which is unspoiled by the white culture and modern civilization. The close and harmonious relationship with nature is reflected in maintaining a simple and natural lifestyle. The author chooses a character from each of the three stages of Morrison's career to examine, such as Pilate in *Song of Solomon*, Son Green in *Tar Baby*, and Convent women in *Paradise*.

In *Song of Solomon*, the relationship between nature and human is fully demonstrated by two opposite types of characters. One is Solomon's father, Macon Dead, who is keen to pursue wealth accumulation while losing the connection with nature. While another typical representative is Solomon's aunt, Pilate, who maintains a close connection with nature, adopting a simple natural way of life. Pilate is the pivotal character in this novel, as Morrison says in an interview, "[s] he was a very large character and loomed very large in the book" (McKay, 1994: 418). In this character, Morrison expresses her idea of communicating with nature and resists against the whites' values to build a uniquely black identity. From the name, Pilate, given by her father Jake, we can see her intrinsic relation with nature:

> [Jake] chose a group of letters that seemed to him strong and

handsome; saw in them a large figure that looked like a tree hanging in some princely but protective way over a row of smaller trees. (*Solomon*, 18)

Her name is related to the image of a tree which is endowed with strength and productive power. The tree image appears repeatedly in this novel, symbolizing Pilate's incarnation of nature. For example, as a girl, she likes to chew pine needles and is smelled "like a forest". Her house at the southside is "backed by four huge pine trees" (27). During Macon's secret visit to her house, seeing Pilate stirring wine pulp and listening to the three female singing songs, Macon identifies her as swaying like a willow over her stirring. Guitar and Milkman also make the same identification for their first impression on her, thinking she looks "like a tall black tree" (39). Pilate not only bears the physical features of trees in nature but also lives a life closely connected with nature. Her name, her dress, her way of life, etc., show her original living state of nature. As a child, Pilate immerses herself in her father's farm and the surrounding woods. She lives a self-sufficient, natural lifestyle with few modern facilities in her home:

Her house sat eighty feet from the sidewalk and was backed by four huge pine trees, from which she got the needles she stuck into her mattress. Seeing the pine trees started him thinking about her mouth; how she loved, as a girl, to chew pine needles and as a result smelled even then like a forest. (23)

There is no electricity or gas in her house. They use candles and kerosene lamps for light, and use wood and coal to cook meals; they also pump water with a pipeline from a well. They live a frugal, casual life:

No meal was ever planned or balanced or served. Nor was there any gathering at the table. Pilate might bake hot bread and each one of them would eat it with butter whenever she felt like it. Or there might be grapes, leftover from the winemaking, or peaches for days on end. If one of them bought a gallon of milk they drank it until it was gone. If another got a half bushel of tomatoes or a dozen ears of corn, they ate them until they were gone too. They ate what they had or came across or had a craving for. Profits from their wine-selling evaporated like seawater in a hot wind—going for junk jewelry for Hagar, Reba's gifts to men, and he didn't know what all. (24–25)

Pilates cares little about material life, loves nature and simplicity, and is faithful to her emotions. She is wild by nature and does not depend on other's criteria to define her own. Nature gives her strength to be integrated and confident. Although Pilate does not have material prosperity like his brother, Macon Dead, her spiritual life is rich and colorful. She tries to avoid the influence of the industrial society and maintains a simple lifestyle with less material desire.

After a quarrel with her brother, Pilate heads for the south and begins her wandering life. In the harsh environment, Pilate has developed different kinds of survival skills in nature and has become a strong, brave, and independent woman. She travels in different states with the guidance of her geography book. She gets strength and consolation from nature which gives her full inner satisfaction in her life. Confucius also believes that human gains spiritual guidance and power from the natural world to support themselves, as he says, "The wise delight in water; the humane delight in mountains." (Annping, 2014: 128) It means wise people are drawn to rivers or streams because they bring to mind great things, like the living impulse, a forward motion, clearness, purity, and unfathomable depth. And humane people have a deep connection with mountains because they are still and stable; they do not move but they are home to grass and trees, birds and animals, and all living things. Humane people find a home in the mountains, and they are like the mountains, because they are contemplative and their lives are reflective. Water and mountain in the natural world endow great spiritual power to human, which illustrates the close connection between human and nature. Pilate insists on the most natural way of living and gains strength from nature to deal with the predicament in life. That is the reason why Morrison shapes her as the spiritual leader to Milkman's self-growth and the black community.

Turning to Morrison's second writing stage, *Tar Baby* is the first novel of this period. Morrison creates characters that truly love nature and harmoniously coexist with other creatures in the natural world. As the representative of nature and the black culture, Son Green appears to be the uppermost force that intensifies the harmony between nature and human. The novel starts with Son Green coming from water, indicating his close relationship with nature. Morrison describes Son coming out of the sea, lands on the island, and survives. He is familiar with water, after he jumps ship, the sea just "like the hand of an insistent woman" (*Tar Baby*, 2), pushing him away from land. As Morrison describes Son in the novel,

> The water was so soft and warm that it was up to his armpits before he realizes he was in it. Quickly he brought his knees to his chest and shot forward. He swam well. At each fourth stroke, he turned skyward and lifted his head to make sure his course was parallel to the shore but away. Although his skin blended well with the dark waters, he was careful not to lift his arms too high above the waves. (1)

Son swims in the ocean, and his skin blends well with the dark waters. As we have mentioned in the previous part, water in nature bestows great power and strength to human. Here, Son also gets supernatural power from water, which gives him strength to survive the big ocean. The water lady, the mistress of the ocean, pushes him into another direction of a small boat floating on the river,

> When he tore open the water in front of him, he felt a gentle but firm pressure along his chest, stomach, and down his thighs. Like the land of an

insistent woman, it pushed him ... Just as suddenly the water-lady removed her hand and the man swam toward the boat anchored in the blue water and not the green. (4–5)

In the ocean, Son lets the water carry him for a while instead of struggling with it violently. Soon he is pushed by the water and swims to the boat anchored in the blue water to the island. It seems that it is a natural force that leads him to the island to rescue the degenerated natural environment and people there.

Green is the color of nature, which means that he is the son of nature. He has the black skin, vigorous figure, "spaces, mountains, savannas—all those were in his forehead and eyes" (159). "There he [Son] stood in mauve silk pajamas, his skin as dark as a riverbed." (113) And his hair is alive just as Morrison said, "Black people's hair, in any case, left alone and untended it was like foliage and from a distance, it looked like nothing less than the crown of a deciduous tree." (154) "His smile was always a surprise like a sudden rustle of wind across the savanna of his face." (181) Morrison adopts a lot of vivid description of Son's appearance and characteristics to illustrate his close relationship with nature. Moreover, there are some animal characteristics in him. Like he is "burrowed in his plate-like an animal" (133) and grunting in monosyllables, sipping from his saucer and wiping up a salad dressing with his bread, he is no wild boar, as Jadine usually uses the word "animal" to describe him. "I know you are an animal because I smell you." (79) For Son, nature is the only place where he feels at home. In an interview with Nellie Mckay, Toni Morrison identifies Son Green as a representative of some aspects of "the black culture, the black community that seems lost to our modern ways of life" (Mckay, 1994: 148), it means Son maintains the natural way of living and is not assimilated into modernization.

While staying in a modern New York hotel waiting for Jadine, Son feels so estranged from the city life, "The trouble he'd had the night he checked in was representative of how estranged he felt from these new people" (217). Here, Son realizes his resistance of the city life and is eager to go back to simple natural life. Morrison writes, "He needed the blood-clot heads of the bougainvillea, the simple green rage of the avocado; the fruit of the banana trees puffed up and stiff like the fingers of gouty kings." (220) All these push him to go back to the natural world and run away from the uncomfortable modern city. Son chooses to leave New York at the end of the novel. Morrison describes Son's desire to return to nature with four repeated sentences in four different paragraphs, "He insisted on Eloe" (218), "But he insisted on Eloe" (221), "Still he insisted on Eloe" (223), and "Yet he insisted on Eloe" (228). Here, Morrison shows Son's close contact with his hometown, Eloe, and his strong desire to immerse with nature. Even Morrison herself states that "the suggestion at the end, when the trees step back to make way for a certain kind of man, is that Nature is urging him to join them" (Mckay, 1994:150). Morrison describes her love for nature and sense of natural protection through Son's eyes, which echoes the Confucian view of nature.

In addition, Son believes that "Wilderness wasn't wild anymore or threatening; wildlife needed human protection to existing at all" (221). It is an expression of Son's love for nature and his awareness of protecting nature. He has a sincere love for nature and seems to have the ability to communicate with plants and animals. Son seems to "know all about plants" and makes use of the knowledge to solve problems in life. For instance, Valerian builds a greenhouse to grow northern flowers on the island, but the flowers don't blossom at all, which bothers Valerian for a long time. When Son watches the flowers, he shakes the flowers "with thumb and middle finger flicked the stems hard as though they were naughty students", and tells Valerian that "they just need jacking up" (146). Afterward, Valerian's plants begin to thrive under Son's care. Another example is the ants in Valerine's greenhouse. Son tells him to put some mirrors outside the door, because "Ants won't come near a mirror" (147), and it proves to be effective. Son also tells Ondine to put banana leaves in the shoes to soothe her foot pain. Son seems to understand everything about the natural world and is endowed with supernatural power from nature. In a conversation with Robert Stepto, Morrison claims that "there is an incredible amount of magic and feistiness in black men that nobody has been able to wipe out. But everybody has tried" (Robert, 1991:17). Morrison repeatedly describes Son as a natural character as well as a magic man. Through describing the characteristics and behaviors of Son, Morrison shows his close connection with nature. Coming to the third stage of her writing career, Morrison continues to explore the relationship between human and nature. The following section takes the first novel of this period as an example to illustrate Morrison's idea.

Women and nature always form an intimate relationship in literary works, and *Paradise* is no exception. Women, like nature, are in a disadvantaged position in society. Nature has been exploited by human beings to make profits, and women also have been deprived of basic rights in the patriarchal society. Moreover, both nature and women bear the responsibility of reproduction, as nature is the basis of life in the universe and women take the obligation of bearing children. Besides, women generally play the role of a comforter and listener in family, which is similar to the healing function of nature. Nature is also the asylum for women, protecting them from the persecution of patriarchal society, healing the hurt inflicted by men, and providing strength for living. Nature and women share the same destiny and are closely connected. In *Paradise*, Morrison depicts women in Convent who maintain the natural lifestyle and seek a way out of the persecution from the patriarchal society.

Contrary to people in Ruby Town, the Convent women seem like living in nature. When the Ruby men rush into Convent, they find:

> Each woman sleeps not in a bed, like normal people, but in a hammock. Other than that, and except for a narrow desk or an end table, there is no additional furniture. No clothes in the closets, of course, since the women wore no-fit dirty dresses and nothing you could honestly call shoes. But there

are strange things nailed or taped to the walls or propped in a corner. (*Paradise*, 8)

The Convent women are "surrounded by corn, buffalo grass, clover and approached by a dirt track barely seen from the road. The mansion-turned-Convent was there long before the town" (11). Unlike the tidy Ruby, the Convent is:

Messy—the floor in one of them is covered with food-encrusted dishes, dirty cups, its bed invisible under a hill of clothes; another room sports two rocking chairs full of dolls; a third the debris and smell of a heavy drinker—but normal at least. (9)

They maintain the simplest way of living just like in wild nature. Moreover, women in the Convent make a living by themselves, and they also take the responsibility of providing food for the Ruby people. Apart from the material supplies they provide, they also provide shelter and refuge for other people in need regardless of race and gender. They give the traumatized people spiritual comfort and guidance, which is just like the function of the natural world. There is a detailed description of nature's healing function in *Paradise*:

The rain's perfume was stronger north of Ruby, especially at the Convent, where thick white clover and Scotch broom colonized every place but the garden. Mavis and Pallas, aroused from sleep by its aroma, rushed to tell Consolata, Grace, and Seneca that longer for rain finally comes. Gathered in the kitchen door, first, they watched; then they stuck out their hands to fell. It was like lotion fingers so they entered it and let it pour like a balm on their shaved hands and upturned faces ... If there were any recollections of a recent warning or intimation of harm, the irresistible rain washed them away. (283)

The Convent women dance in the rain and embrace nature; their miseries are washed away by the rain. It seems that the rain has some magic power that cures their sorrow and pain. For that moment, they acquire authentic freedom and become truly liberated people. Evidently, the harmonious relationship between Convent women and nature is of great importance to their mental and physical recovery. And they pass love and care to other people in trouble. In summary, Pilate, Son and Convent women are representatives of Morrison's characters who maintain a simple, natural lifestyle to keep a close connection with nature. Except for the natural way of living, Morrison also depicts some characters who gain spiritual and moral support from nature to prove the necessity of keeping a harmonious relationship with nature.

2.2.2 Spiritual Support from Nature

Human beings are a part of the natural world, and nature is the final place for human to return to. In Morrison's novels, natural images have been adopted extensively to illustrate her observation of the relationship between human and nature. For instance, images of plants have always occupied an important position in her works, from which people could get divine revelation and power in life. Human beings could gain a sense of self-love, and finally establish self-identity with integrated moral and value system. In her works, Morrison depicts several characters who get strength and courage from nature, and finally complete their self-growth from destruction to rebirth. In this section, the author adopts Morrison's three novels, *Song of Solomon*, *Beloved*, and *A Mercy* from each of her three stages of writing, to demonstrate nature's function in human's trauma recovery and self-identity reconstruction.

Song of Solomon centers around Milkman's journey from the Northern middle class home to his ancestral home in the south. Morrison describes him as an emotionally isolated, psychologically alienated African American man who has grown up in the industrial northern city. Though he is thirty-one years old, he still lives an aimless, selfish, and irresponsible life under the influence of his father. He cares about nobody in the family or in the community. Still living in his parents' home, collecting rent for his father, Milkman has yet to reach emotional and social maturity. Though he lives a wealthy and abundant life, his spiritual world is barren and empty. His poverty is spiritual, not material. As the only son in the family, he indulges himself in the sense of self-centered. Once Milkman says that "I live and let live" (*Solomon*, 216), which means he cares nothing except his own life. To his sisters, Lena and Corinthians, he has never taken any notice of their life and lives with them as if they are strangers. Just as Lena says, Milkman has been "peeing on" the family all of his life. Moreover, his incestuous love with Hagar, at last, leads to Hagar's craziness.

Because he has been fed up with "Lena's anger, Corinthians' loose and uncombed hair, matching her slack lips, Ruth's stepped-up surveillance, his father's bottomless greed, Hagar's hollow eyes" (220), Milkman wants to run away from the dull, repressed life desperately and look for gold. He leaves from northern Michigan to the south, where the environment is quite different from the northern industrial city. When Milkman is in the north, he always feels tension and uneasiness and looks back when he walks. However, after he moves from the northern modern city to the southern village of his ancestor's hometown, he starts to change. In the south, human beings and everything in the natural world are intimate and communicate with each other. Morrison describes that before the development of human society, human and nature are originally harmonious and interdependent with each other:

> Language in the time when men and animals did talk to one another, when a man could sit down with an ape and the two converse; when a tiger and a man could share the same tree, and each understood the other; when men ran with wolves, not from or after them. And he was hearing it in the Blue Ridge Mountains under a sweet gum tree. And if they could talk to

animals, and the animals could talk to them, what didn't they know about human beings? Or the earth itself, for that matter. (206)

In the process of hunting, Milkman has a close contact with nature. He begins to realize that money, car, fame, suit and leather shoes, and all the material life he enjoyed before has become a stumbling block to his self-growth. In the moors, lying on the ground under the moonlight, Milkman begins to reflect on his life. He reflects on his past behaviors toward his parents, his sisters, Hagar, Guitar, and to other people around him, eventually realizes his ignorance and vanity:

> They were troublesome thoughts, but they wouldn't go away. Under the moon, on the ground, alone, with not even the sound of baying dogs to remind him that he was with other people, his self—the cocoon that was "personality"—gave way. He could barely see his own hand, and couldn't see his feet. He was only his breath, coming slower now, and his thoughts. The rest of him had disappeared. So the thoughts came, unobstructed by other people, by things, even by the sight of himself. (205)

We see that when Milkman stays in the wilderness and has a direct contact with the natural world, he is able to look at his life clearly and contemplate the meaning of life. Nature empowers him with spiritual nourishment and helps him gain the inner peace and meaning of life. Moreover, in nature, the friendship of other African Americans eases his alienation from the black community. After this hunting experience, when he walks on the southern ground:

> [Milkman] really laughing and he found himself exhilarated by simply walking the earth. Walking it as he belonged on it; like his legs were stalks, tree trunks, a part of his body that extended down into the rock and soil, and were comfortable there—on the earth and on the place where he walked. And he did not limp. (207)

At this moment, he feels the power of nature is nourishing his body and soul as well, even his limp foot does not limp at all. Nature not only saves his soul but also heals his physical injures. Milkman comes to understand he should be responsible for himself and other people. Focusing on the significance of nature in Milkman's growth, Ann Imbrie (1993: 74) suggests that "Milkman underwent education in the primitive, 'natural' countryside and returned to the city with more understanding and acceptance of "his human responsibilities". Milkman has retrieved his responsibility and humanity as a human being through nature's guidance. And he successfully changes himself from a selfish and indifferent man into a helpful and mature grown-up. Just like Catherine Carr Lee describes Solomon as:

> His journey into the black south strips him of superficial external moorings and submerges him in the communal and spiritual culture of his larger family. With his initiation, he moves from a passive, irresponsible, ignorance to an active, authentic, and liberating participation in the corporate life of the black community. (Lee, 1998: 110)

His trip to the south begins as a selfish quest for gold, and his escape turns to a quest for knowledge of his ancestry history and identity. Although his journey ends with no gold, he finally gets knowledge about the history of his ancestors and the black culture. It is nature that endows him with the ability to think about the root of his culture and his meaningless life, and it is nature that gives him the strength to spiritual maturity. At the end of the novel, Milkman realizes what he should do to be an upright human being. Through the story of Milkman's spiritual growth, Morrison shows the healing function of nature and demonstrates the necessity of keeping a harmonious and close relationship with nature in the process of self-identity and moral construction.

Morrison endeavors to show that nature is the spiritual home to African

Americans, from where they gain comfort and courage to struggle with the miserable life in the ruthless society. The protagonist of *Beloved*, Sethe, is another typical character adopted by Morrison to show her concerns about the relationship between human and nature. *Beloved*, one of Morrison's most famous novels and has attracted many critics' attention. In "Selfhood, and Community: Psychoanalysis and Discourse *in Beloved*" (1993), Jennifer Fitzgerald discusses the narrative strategies and female discourse concerning the self-construction of Sethe in *Beloved*. It holds that Sethe's construction of self-identity is connected with her strong desire for independence. Elizabeth Ann Beaulieu, in her *Black Women Writers and the American Neo-Slave Narrative: Femininity Unfettered* (1999), studies the gender politics in *Beloved*. In "Trauma and Collective Memory in Toni Morrison's *Beloved* and *A Mercy*" (2015), C. L. Shilaja states that the plots of her novels explore the various ways in which trauma is present and alive among black characters. It also emphasizes the processes through which her characters search, share, and rememorize their distinct cultural memories upon which to build an identity. The above-mentioned criticisms study *Beloved* from different perspectives, while this book tries to examine it from the relationship between human and nature.

In *Beloved*, Morrison describes the close relationship between nature and human through Sethe, Denver, Paul D, and Baby Suggs. When Sethe is a slave in Sweet Home, she is tortured by the white owner, Schoolteacher. He takes Sethe as an animal and keeps a record of her behavior as a measure of "scientific" experiment. The cruelest thing that Schoolteacher does to Sethe is to beat her on the back with cowhide. The scars on Sethe's back are like a "chokecherry tree", which not only causes her physical pain but also leaves her permanent psychological trauma. To ease her pain in Sweet Home, Sethe tries to seek comfort and a sense of belonging from the natural world. For example, she gains strength and support from plants, as written by Morrison:

[Sethe] had to bring a fistful of salsify into Mrs. Garner's kitchen every day just to be able to work in it, feel like some part of it was hers, because she wanted to love the work she did, to take the ugly out of it, and the only way she could feel at home on Sweet Home was if she picked some pretty growing thing and took it with her. (*Beloved*, 32)

It is clear to see that Sethe finds comfort and consolation from the living plants during her slave life. The living things give her life and hope to live in the cruel society, and she gains a sense of security and belonging from the natural world. What is more, after she escapes from Sweet Home to 124 House Bluestone Road, Sethe's mother-in-law, Baby Suggs tries very hard to help Sethe to recover from the physical and psychological injures. Suggs takes pretty good care of Sethe in 124 House and gives her courage and love to encounter the injures. Sethe finds a sense of security and belonging in the house where is a "cheerful, buzzing house where Baby Suggs, holy, loved, cautioned, fed, chastise and soother. When not one but two pots simmered on the stove; where the lamp burned all night long" (87). Sethe recovers soon in the warm family environment with Baby Suggs. The natural surroundings of the house also help Sethe to recover from her past traumas. The Clearing—a wide open place in the woods where Suggs preached gives Sethe spiritual guidance. Surrounded by the natural environment of 124 House and Suggs' mother-like love, Sethe recovers from her physical and psychological pain bit by bit. In the end, she succeeds in restoring her self-consciousness as a human being.

Baby Suggs plays an important role in Sethe's trauma recovery, and Morrison depicts her as a spiritual leader in the black community. Baby Suggs spends sixty years in slavery life and suffers a lot of pain physically and psychologically. Her whole life is full of sorrow, "Anybody Baby Suggs knew, let alone loved, who hadn't run off of been hanged, got rented out, loaned out, bought up, brought back, stored up, mortgaged, won, stolen or seized" (23). When she lives in the Sweet Home, she is treated as a sexual toy for the white men. And she is also a reproduction machine for her owner to increase the slave numbers. Just as Angela Davis (2000: 125) says, "In the eyes of the slaveholder, slave women were not mothers at all, they were simply instruments guaranteeing the growth of the slave labor force." Although Suggs has seven children, she only watches them being taken away one after another. Like other black women, she is deprived of the right of motherhood as a human being.

However, Baby Suggs keeps a positive attitude toward her life under the slavery system. After retrieving freedom, she comes to 124 Bluestone Road that is surrounded by nature and far away from the slavery system. Suggs is the first African American woman living there independently. Her house becomes a place for other people gathering together to get solace, relief, and support. She helps them in the neighborhood and becomes "an unchurched preacher, one who visited pulpits and opened her great heart to those who could use it" (87). Suggs's realization of spiritual independence has closely related to nature, as she gains strength from nature and acts as the spiritual leader to other people there. She tells them to love themselves and to cherish every part of their body, "Love your heart. For this is the prize" (89). It is in this natural space called Clearing that other African Americans release their depression and pain caused by the slavery system. Nature gives them a sense of existence and belonging as well as consolation and strength. In *Beloved*, Sethe and Suggs' experience show that nature functions as an instrument to give courage and support to human, and human and nature are closely connected.

Morrison once explained her motivation for writing *A Mercy*, "I wanted to get to a place before slavery was equated with race. Whether they were black or white was less important than what they owned or what their power was." Morrison holds the view that racial discrimination is not only about the black people, but also exists within other races. In this novel, Morrison's concerns change from the black people to the whole humankind. In "Maternal Love/ Maternal Violence: Inventing Ethics in Toni Morrison's *A Mercy*" (2014), Naomi

Morgenstern discusses the ethics of the black maternity and whether the decision made by the black mother is right or wrong under the circumstances of no power. The black maternity is an important theme of Morrison's works, and violent maternal love always is a heated topic for discussion. The author agrees with Naomi's opinion. Though it is brutal and lack of ethics to commit violence in maternal love, it is understandable that the slave mothers use violence to protect their children from the cruel slavery system. In this section, the author turns to examine the relationship between human and nature in this novel.

In *A Mercy*, Morrison depicts several women on Jacob's farm, who regard nature as shelter and gain tranquility from nature. They respect nature with appreciation and gratitude and maintain a harmonious relationship with nature. A notable example is Florens, who is abandoned not only by her mother when she is young but also by a blacksmith when she grows up. She has gone through a series of physical and spiritual wound by these experiences and thinks that nobody loves her at all. Florens lives a miserable life without any happiness. When the hostess of the farm, Rebekka, falls sick, Florens is sent to seek the blacksmith to cure her master. On the road, Florens is attracted by the natural beauty that pervades everywhere. A little green in raw weather gives her happiness, enabling her to observe the woods she is passing through with an appreciative eye. She observes that "the sky is the color of currants" and "the moonlight is young" (*Mercy*, 41). The beautiful natural scenes arouse Florens' love of the natural environment, relax her mood, and cheer up her spirit. When she has to stay overnight in the forests, she finds "the old pines are very big. And one is a good cover" (42). In the embrace of these trees, Florens feels safe when she stays in the pitch-dark and frigid wilderness. Just like Muir says:

> Actually, ramble in the woods of the God is much safer than travel on the dark road and stay at home ... if a man does not want to explore other things, he, then, can seek security in the forests. (Muir, 1981: 1-2)

For Florens, the wilderness is much safer than the farm where she lives. Nature gives her a sense of security and belonging.

Through describing Florens' psychology stirred by the light green branches and leaves, Morrison reasserts that the natural world give people enlightenment in thought and mold their spirit. At night, sitting in the open field, Florens often has her eyes on the night sky be sprinkled with innumerable stars, listening to Lina narrating stories. In nature, Florens forgets her pain, regains inner enrichment, and retains her peace of mind. The beauty of nature is converted into an inside impetus propping up her spirit. Under the umbrella of nature, Florens' heart becomes peaceful and "fell excited among the sublime appearances of nature; and be in a tranquil state of calm observation in the appreciation of nature's beauty" (Kant, 1999: 97). It is nature that makes her feel "full" and "free" in spirit; and she worries and fears no more to her future life. At last she deems that "the soles of my feet are as hard as cypress" (161), which means that she has gained the strength to face up to the hardships and miseries in the future.

Another character is Lina, an Indian girl, suffering a lot since childhood. When she is very young, pestilence breaks out in the village where she lives and almost all the villagers died in the end. Later Lina is adopted by some Presbyterians who give her the name Lina. Then she is sold to Jacob as a maidservant. On the farm of Jacob, she sleeps with chickens and lives in the cowshed. Lina lives a life full of distress and weariness. Lonesomeness, exhaustion, and resentfulness make her feel depressed. In order to survive, she blends herself with the natural world to seek spiritual comfort, courage, and confidence to face up to the difficult situation in life. "She cawed with birds, chatted with plants, spoke to squirrels, sang to the cow, and opened her mouth to rain ... She also danced in the moonlight." (49) In Lina's eyes, animals and plants are as alive as human and human should love and communicate with them. Confucianism "unity of Heaven and human" also holds that all things in nature have life, and should be treated with "benevolence" (ren, 仁). The basic meaning of benevolence is love for others. Its extended meaning refers to the harmonious relations among all the creatures in the natural world. It requires mutual respect and love between human and other species. Lina's behavior corresponds with benevolence advocated by Confucianism. Through communicating with nature, treating other species equally, and perceiving the beauty of the natural world, Lina casts her impulsiveness aside and retrieves tranquility of mind, and finally gains the enrichment and sublimation in spirit.

In this chapter, the author describes the disharmonious and harmonious relationship between human and nature in Morrison's novels. She shows human destruction and domination of nature as well as alienation from nature by characters in *Paradise, Love, A Mercy, Song of Solomon, and Tar Baby*. In addition, Morrison advocates the natural lifestyle adopted by several of her characters, such as Pilate, Son Green, and Convent women in *Song of Solomon, Tar Baby, and Paradise*. They act as the spiritual leader of the black culture with spiritual richness and inner peacefulness. What is more, through Milkman's spiritual growth in *Song of Solomon*, Sethe and Suggs' trauma recovery in *Beloved*, Lena and Florens' spiritual consolation in *A Mercy*, Morrison exhibits that human attains strength and support from nature to realize their self-growth and achieve their spiritual wholeness. From what has been examined above, nature occupies an important place in Morrison's novels. She holds that human should return to the natural world, and establish a harmonious relationship with nature. It is obvious that Morrison and "unity of Heaven and human" emphasize the importance of nature in human spiritual growth and completeness. Human should protect nature and maintain a harmonious coexistence with nature to realize the sustainable development of human society. So far this book has focused on the relationship between human and nature in Morrison's novels. The following chapter moves on to discuss the relationship between human and society in her novels.

3

Relationship Between Human and Society

Industrialization not only destroys the relationship between human and nature but also ruins humanity and leads to a distorted relationship between people. The harmonious relationship between people is destroyed by imperialism, colonization, and discrimination. People can't achieve self-realization and consequently lose their self-identity in life. All these issues mentioned above have become the concerns of Morrison's novels. Morrison also explores ways to construct a harmonious relationship among people regardless of gender, race, and class difference. She strongly opposes androcentrism, ethnocentrism, and colonialism, and various forms of social discrimination and inequality. By analyzing the conflicts and contradictions among people in society, Morrison demonstrates her preliminary exploration of building a harmonious society.

As an African American, Morrison confronted institutionalized racism in segregated Washington. D. C. when she enrolled at Howard University in 1949. It was the first time that Morrison faced segregation in a different form than what she'd grown up with in Ohio. As an African American literature professor at Howard University, Dana Williams said, "It was the first time that she wasn't able to try on clothes in a store. Even when she was working full-time, she wasn't able to get credit." Morrison witnessed the suppressed life of African Americans in the white-dominated society. The Civil Rights Movement struggled for social justice that took place mainly during the 1950s and 1960s for the black Americans to gain equal rights in American society. But the discrimination against the black Americans didn't end, and they continued to endure the devastating effects of racism. Morrison pays more attention to the unequal and disharmonious relations between people in society. She is also concerned about the relationship between people in the family, as family is the basic unit that makes up society. Morrison attaches great importance to the social relations between people, which includes the interpersonal link between an individual with his family members and with other people in society.

In her novels, the characters usually suffer some ethical crisis because of their distorted familial and social relations. The failure of constructing a harmonious relationship with other people in life leads to the incompleteness of one's self-identity. Through these characters' life, Morrison emphasizes the importance of maintaining a healthy relationship with other people in family and society. As presented in the introduction, Confucian "unity of Heaven and human" also proposes to establish a harmonious relationship with family members and other people in society. As Confucius said, "A youngster should be filial within his home and respectful of elders. When outside, he should be careful and trustworthy, broadly caring for people at large, and should cleave to those who are *ren* (benevolence). If he has energy left over, he may study the refinements of culture." (Annping, 2014: 37) What Confucius stresses in this saying is the importance of grasping the fundamentals of human relationships in family and then in society. In this chapter, the author turns to examine the interrelationship between people within the context of family and society. With regard to the relation between family members, this book focuses on the parent-child relationship. In terms of the relationship with others in society, the author examines it from the distorted and harmonious interrelationship displayed in Morrison's novels.

3.1 Relationship Between Parents and Children

Confucian "unity of Heaven and human" proposes that family is the basic unit of society, and it is the important place for children's growth. The relationship between parents and children has a great influence on children's physical and mental development. Parents are the first teachers to children in children's moral education and well-being. As Wade Horn states, "Parents are the world's greatest experts on their children. They are their children's first and most important caregivers, teachers, and providers." (Buss & Herman, 2003: 83) Parents bear the responsibility to raise and educate children. According to *The Book of Rites*, a child would spend nearly all his time with his parents in the first ten years of his life. Learning the appropriate way of showing his love toward his parents will prepare him to be respectful of other people when he is outside home. In addition, Confucianism holds the view that a harmonious family environment helps the children to form a stable and reasonable personality, whereas a twisted one would have a negative influence on children's personality development. With regard to the parent-child relations, the author focuses on father-child and mother-child relationships. In her novels, Morrison shows the appalling truth of the absence of familial love in African-American families. In the next section, the book examines the distorted paternal love described in Morrison's *The Bluest Eye*, *Song of Solomon*, and *God Help the Child*.

3.1.1 Distorted Paternal Love

The parent-child relationship is not merely a kind of close ties but a manifestation of ethical responsibility and obligation. Parents should care about the growth and education of their children and, in turn, children also have obligations to support their parents. It is not only a demand for social ethics but also a moral criterion in family. Father is always the symbol of authority and takes the responsibility of protecting and educating children. Some critics believe that father plays a central role in children's growth. A healthy father-child relationship helps the child to build his confidence and independence. However, the paternal love depicted by Morrison is usually absent or deformed. By portraying the family in her novels, Morrison describes the ethical predicament of parents and children, and claims for a loving and responsible relationship between them. In

Morrison's first novel, *The Bluest Eye*, Cholly's paternal love for his daughter, Pecola, is shocking and twisted.

In *The Bluest Eye*, the relationships between spouses and between parents and children are alienated and detached. Cholly and Pauline are the typical couple who are influenced by the alienated life in the northern city. When they live in the south, they love each other. Though Pauline is limp at that time, Cholly takes her limp as something special. However, after moving to the northern city, Cholly fails to meet the increasing material needs of Pauline and the couple become indifferent to each other. Quarrels and domestic violence are common in their family. What's worse, both fail to take responsibility as parents to their children, especially to their daughter, Pecola, who is the biggest victim of this family. Because of her black skin, Pecola is disdained even by her parents. As a mother, Pauline forbids Pecola to call her mother but Mr. Breedlove. She pays no attention to Pecola's growth. Even after knowing she is raped by her father, Pauline blames Pecola rather than showing concern for her. The indifference and ruthlessness of her parents cause great harm the the formation of Pecola's personality.

As the central member of the family, Cholly should bear the responsibility of taking care of his children and family, but he fails. His irresponsibility is also related to his tragic experience in childhood. His father Samson Fuller was indulged in gambling and drinking every day. Samson deserted Cholly and his mother to abandon the responsibility as a husband and father. Then Cholly was raised by his Aunt Jimmy after his mother dumped him in a dustbin after birth. After his aunt died, when he was fourteen, Cholly embarked on the journey to find his father. Unfortunately, after Cholly found his father, he was driven away brutally by his father once again because the unfamiliar boy disturbed his dice game, "Tell that bitch she gets her money. Now, get the fuck outta my face!" (*The Bluest Eye*, 142) Due to his father's selfish and irresponsible behaviors, Cholly does not get a positive example and influence, let alone the knowledge of paternal love. His father's abandonment not only causes great psychological trauma on

Cholly but also affects his ability to conduct his paternal role as a father to his children. Cholly does not know how to raise a child, "He could not even understand what such a relationship should be" (26). Naturally, he is unable to bear the responsibility of taking care of his children and educating them on morality. "As thus, Cholly's absence of concern and love and the behaviors without moral bounds inevitably result in the subsequent traumatic event." (Gillespie, 2007:51) Cholly's distorted paternal love for Pecola is largely caused by the lack of education of being a father.

Confucianism believes that human nature is "neither good nor evil", and it is influenced by living environment and moral education. And parents are supposed to provide righteous moral guidance and set a good example for their children to become an authentic human being. Parents' education is required in children's formation of characteristics and values. For example, the virtue of benevolence is obtained through education and cultivation:

> [Benevolence] is a quality about one's caring disposition toward others that has to be developed and fully embodied before a biological person can become an authentic human being. It must be embodied, and not merely understood and followed as a universal principle or imperative. For this reason, it is a matter of cultivation rather than gaining propositional knowledge, and by its nature unsuitable for conceptual formulation. (Ni, 2016: 61)

Parents need to bear the responsibility of guiding and educating their children in morality cultivation. Owing to his irresponsible and selfish father, Cholly shows his distorted paternal love to his daughter, Pecola.

Except for the negative influence of his father, Cholly's failure as a father is also due to his sense of inferiority in society, which is caused by the white's discrimination against African Americans. Cholly and Pauline leave the southern hometown to the north after the Civil War. However, their expectations of a better life in the north shatter. In the white-dominated society, the white Americans are superior and the black Americans are inferior. Consequently, when he encounters humiliation and discrimination from the white people, Cholly lets off his anger towards his wife and children. He quarrels with his wife and vents his anger on his daughter Pecola. What's worse, he resorts to alcohol to relieve his depression and frustration. One day, when he returns home after being heavily drunken, Cholly finds Pecola doing the dishes in the kitchen. At that time, Pecola's images and actions trigger his emotion and lead to his animal-like behavior towards his daughter. Morrison depicts Cholly's psychological activity as follows:

> Cholly saw her dimly and could not tell what he saw or what he felt. Then he became aware that he was uncomfortable; next, he felt the discomfort dissolve into pleasure. The sequence of his emotions was revulsion, guilt, pity, and then love. His revulsion was a reaction to her young, helpless, hopeless presence. (161)

Wandering between love and disgust, Cholly intends to strangle his daughter but in a tender means. At this moment, he watches Pecola doing the chores by the sink, "one foot scratching the back of the calf with her toe" (127), which reminds him of the sweet memories in Kentucky with his wife. He is so puzzled to see the distinction between his wife and daughter, sex and love. Tragically, he confuses his paternal love with sexual desire. He chooses to convey such a helpless and distorted parental love to his daughter. Just as Morrison says, "That his love towards his daughter and the mentality that he cannot remove her pain. By then, all he offers is only the hug and rape itself." (Claudia, 1984: 125) His rape of Pecola reflects the total failure of his role as a father. All ethical rules and family responsibility have been completely discarded. "It seems that his soul slips down to the guts." (128) What is worse, he chooses to run away from home at last. Cholly's distorted paternal love and ethical dilemma of incest with his daughter not only destroy him but also ruin Pecola's whole life. As a father, Cholly should be the person who protects, loves, and educates Pecola. However, he is irresponsible and ruthless, and even rapes her. Morrison depicts Cholly as a typical father who shows a distorted paternal love and fails to bear the responsibility of a father.

In *Song of Solomon*, the dominant love of Macon Dead towards his son Milkman and his two daughters also causes great harm to his children. And the abnormal family environment made by him hinders the physical and psychological growth of his children.

Macon Dead is a businessman who is ruthless and indifferent to other people. The only thing he cares about is money. "Owning, building, acquiring that was his life, his future, his present, and all the history he knew." (*Solomon*, 222) He is a tyrant in his family, dominating the life of Milkman and his two daughters. He plans his children's future without considering the real needs and the moral education of them. When Milkman is twelve years old, Macon teaches him to bear the value of money accumulation, and asks him to collect money by extreme means. He tells Milkman that, "Let me tell you right now the one important thing you'll ever need to know: to own things. And let the things you own own other things. Then you'll own yourself and other people too." (55) As a father, he only teaches Milkman the industrial value of accumulating wealth rather than the value of being an upright person. Milkman works for his father in the way as his father wants. "And you're my son. And you will do what I tell you to do. With or without explanations, as long as your feet are under my table, you'll do in this house what you are told." (40) Macon cares nothing about what Milkman wants but asks him to live as he wants.

As to his two daughters, Macon is indifferent to their growth and life. everyday Lena and Corinthians:

Sitting like big baby dolls before a table heaped with scraps of red velvet.

> Every day, the two girls made roses in the afternoon. Bright, lifeless roses that laid in peck baskets for months until the specialty buyer at Gerhardt's sent Freddie the janitor over to tell the girls that they could use another gross. (10)

The two girls stay in the room making rose petals though they are both over 40, and they never have a chance to contact other people outside. Macon makes his two daughters live a loveless, dull life just like the red velvet rosy petals they make. It is not until Corinthians goes to work as a maid of Miss Michael-Mary that:

> [Corinthians] knows nothing about being a human, even she is forty-two-year-old, she does not do anything except making the rose petals all day long; she finds herself life-meaning in the poetess Miss Michael-Mary Graham's house as a maid: "Actually, the work Corinthians did was good for her. In that house, she had what she never had in her own: responsibility." (143)

It is so pathetic for Corinthians to know the meaning of living and responsibility at age forty-two. This is all because of Macon's controlling love. Lena hates her father too, because he regards them as a show-off decoration. Cholly asks them to dress up nicely to stand in front of the poor black men to enjoy their envy. Moreover, Macon fails the responsibility of educating his children with love and respect. He only exerts the controlling power over them which leads them to become defective persons who cannot adjust to society. As to Milkman, under the influence of his father and the distorted family environment, he has no sense of responsibility and concern towards other people.

Milkman is not born with immoral characteristics such as irresponsibility, selfishness, ruthlessness, as the formation of personality and morality is affected by education as well as the external living environment. Mencius asserts the innate goodness of human, believing that it is outward negative influence that causes bad moral character. He says in *Mencius*, "He who exerts his mind to the utmost knows his nature." Another Confucian philosopher Gaozi (告子) advocates the theory of human nature is "neither good nor evil". Here, human nature refers to the inborn attributes of a human being. According to Gaozi, a person's inherent desires reflect no more than physical needs, such as the need for food and sex. Such instincts are irrelevant to ethics, free of good or evil. A person's good or evil traits result from the cultivation and living environment after birth. People who are exposed to good influences tend to do good things. People who live in a bad environment tend to do bad things. Parent's performance in daily life exerts an imperceptible influence on children, including ethical influence. In the period of moral unconsciousness, children are educated and influenced by parents' principles and teachings. Confucius says:

> Learning rituals is no different from learning to be a human. Humans are like raw materials—they need to be carved, chiseled, grounded, and polished to become an authentic person. (Annping, 2014: 43)

The morality of rituals is not something extrinsic to the person, but is the result of transformation and cultivation from parents. Parents should behave with morality and ethics so as to set a virtuous moral example to their children.

Additionally, as a father, Macon should make a harmonious family environment with his wife for their children. However, his indifference makes his wife stunned into stillness. Ruth "began her days stunned into stillness by her husband's contempt and ended them wholly animated by it" (11). The reason why he marries Ruth is to acquire her father's property and become a rich person in the community, "It was because of those keys that he could dare to walk over to that part of Not Doctor Street (it was still Doctor Street then) and approach the most important Negro in the city" (20). Macon has no affection on his wife and even deprives the sex of Ruth, just like Ruth tells Milkman, "I was twenty years old when your father stopped sleeping in the bed with me. That's hard, Macon, very hard. By the time I was thirty thinking I was just afraid I'd die that way" (95). Ruth lives a lonely, oppressed life because of Macon's indifference and oppression. Macon sets a negative example of treating women to Milkman. Milkman becomes an irresponsible person to abandon Hagar only because he tires of her.

The alienation and indifference between family members cause the disintegration of family and loss of self-identity of the children. Morrison insists that a father should not only love and respect the children but also make a harmonious family environment for the children's growth. Moreover, a father should educate children with upright moral education and set a positive example for children. However, what Macon does is exactly the opposite of the role of a father. The same idea is demonstrated by Confucian "unity of Heaven and human". It proposes that everyone in a family should understand and conduct his particular role to make a harmonious family. If parents don't perform these responsibilities to their children, it leads to the destruction of their children's growth physically and psychologically.

The role of father, especially in a society with racial discrimination and alienation, counts a lot for children's healthy growth. Family is the place that provides support and love to a person. And a father bears the responsibility of providing protection and guidance for the children with moral education. However, these are not available to Lula Ann Bridewell, short named as Bride. Bride is the protagonist of *God Help the Child*, and her life is destroyed by absence of paternal love. Her father Louis and mother Sweetness are both high yellow-skinned while Bride is dark blue blackness. Both refuse to admit that Bride inherits the black skin from their own genes. Louis even blames his wife for Bride's Sudanese blackness and suspects whether she is his biological daughter. Neither one could bear the humiliation that Bride's "terrible color" is from any of them. Louis, the father of Bride, is a light-dark porter at rails, who could not stand her blackness after the first glance at her. He isn't a cussing man but bursts out the words surprisingly, "Goddamn! What the hell is this?" and "he never touched her" (*God Help the Child*, 5). He disdains his daughter and treats her like a stranger just because of her dark black skin. What is worse, he does not conduct his role as the supporter and protector of the family and runs away from home. Sweetness complains about Louis' escape as "I told him her blackness must be from his own family—not mine. That's when it got worse, so bad he just up and left" (6). They blame each other for this and finally break their three-year marriage into pieces.

Father plays an important role in nurturing and educating children and ensuring their physical and psychological health. However, Louis escapes from his responsibility as a father. It is tough for Sweetness to raise a child alone, and survival is one of the vital problems for Sweetness. "I don't have to tell you how hard it is being an abandoned wife." (6) Facing both emotional and financial difficulties, Sweetness attributes all the misfortune to Bride's birth and abuses her daughter physically and mentally. Louis' failure to conduct paternal responsibility causes collateral damages to Bride. She never receives any protection or love from her father. In addition, Louis' indifference and neglect of Bride is a kind of emotional abuse to her. Emotional abuse has a vicious influence on the development of a child's mental health, behavior, and self-esteem. It is especially damaging during the critical period of infancy. And the absence of a father's love and education block Bride's spiritual growth, which also causes trauma and her loss of subjectivity. As discussed above, paternal love is essential for children's growth, meanwhile, mother love plays the same important role in children's life and development. The following discussion focuses on the mother-child relationship, which mainly explores an abnormal maternal love in Morrison's novels.

3.1.2 Abnormal Maternal Love

Maternal love is one of the most important themes in Morrison's works.

Mother plays a critical role in the process of children's physical and mental growth, Morrison "believes that before a child can love herself; she must go through the process of being loved and has the sense that she is indeed valuable and deserves to be loved" (Reilly, 2004: 229). Parents are regarded as the first caretakers of children who shape a great influence on children's growth. Except for paternal love, motherhood or maternity is another aspect of family relations. It is widely believed that maternal love is the most selfless love in human life, of which the first duty is to bring up and educate children with a healthy personality. Mother should give their children love and respect, which is vital to the harmony of a family. However, in Morrison's novels, maternal love is either distorted or absent for their children. We find a description of maternal love in all of her novels, and the book selects *The Bluest Eye*, *Beloved*, and *God Help the Child* to discuss, as the protagonists are all little girls.

In *The Bluest Eye*, Pauline's indifference and despise towards her daughter brings fatal damage to Pecola's physical and psychological health. Pauline is a typical African American woman who has internalized the white aesthetic in the white-dominated society. Her self-esteem as an African American has been destroyed by the white beauty standards. In her eyes, the black Americans are inferiors to the white Americans. She turns her hatred to her daughter, who is the biggest victim in the family. When she is pregnant with Pecola, she "talks to herself, she will love her". However, at the first sight of her daughter, the only word she knows is "ugly", "Eyes all soft and wet. Across between a puppy and a dying man, but I knew she was ugly. A head full of pretty hair, but Lord she was ugly" (*The Bluest Eye*, 81). Pauline shows her hatred towards her daughter because the white beauty standard has been rooted in her mind, which implies that she pays no love and care towards Pecola. When Pecola gets her menstruation for the first time, "the only terror is filled with her eyes" and does not know what to do but wonders "if I will die" (27). As a mother, Pauline never teaches her daughter about basic knowledge of living but shows indifference towards Pecola.

Pauline's failure to conduct maternal love is demonstrated vividly after she works in the white Fischer's house. When Pecola spills hot blueberry juice on her leg by accident in the white owner's house, she jumps from the floor because of the burned skin. At this time, Pauline rushes toward Pecola and slaps her heavily without caring about her injury, abusing Pecola, "Crazy guy ... my floor, a mess ... you look ... work ... get out ... right now ... crazy ... my floor, my floor" (87). She concerns more about the floor than her daughter. By contrast, she comforts the scared white daughter with a soft tone. Even when the white girl asks about Pecola, Pauline refuses to admit that Pecola is her daughter. As a mother, Pauline should love and care for her children but what she offers to Pecola is only hurt and hatred. Even when Pecola is raped by her husband, Pauline beats Pecola almost to death without condemning Cholly. When Pecola is raped by her father for a second time, she chooses to keep silent because "my mother would not have been convinced of my suffering at all" (179). The life of Pecola is detached and destroyed by her mother's absence and abnormal love.

Confucianism holds that the most important characteristic of moral consciousness is the ability to distinguish right from wrong. Have been internalized with the white beauty standard, Pauline can't realize the beauty of black skin and can't educate Pecola with an upright attitude of self-love. Gradually, Pecola has convinced herself that her mother hates her because she is black and ugly. She prays to God for a pair of blue eyes like the white girls, which would make her beautiful and loved by her parents. Pecola goes mad after she delivers a dead baby at last. According to Confucian "unity of Heaven and human", blood tie is the strongest link between people. The bond between mother and child is one of the important familial relationships that provide power and love for children to survive in a hostile environment. However, what Pauline offers to Pecola is only hatred and indifference. She not only fails to teach Pecola with correct values but also brings great sufferings to her daughter. Morrison entrenches a kind of maternal failure in this novel and shows that children can't grow up healthily with absence of maternal love.

Unlike the absence of motherhood in *The Bluest Eye*, *Beloved* shows the most appalling expression of maternal love by infanticide. Studies on *Beloved* are various. In "Misery and Company: Sigmund Freud's Presence in Toni Morrison's *Beloved*", Jonathan Halper states:

> Allusions to and uses of psychoanalysis help ground the focus of the story in the internal, it resists what would otherwise be a static and pedantic approach to the issue of slavery and how it has affected both the central family and the United States as a whole. (Halper, 2012: 42)

Another example is the essay "Nobody Could Make It Alone: Fathers and Boundaries in Toni Morrison's *Beloved*", Doreen Fowler states that the importance of the black man is to help the children to recognize their own value and build relationships with others in society. (Fowler, 2011: 19) It affirms the role of father love in children's growth, which the author agrees with. However, the role of maternal love is little touched. The author examines the mother-daughter relationship of *Beloved* in the following section.

In *Beloved*, under the slavery system, the maternal right of slave mothers has been greatly twisted and denied. Sethe conquers unimaginable obstacles to arrive at 124 House, Bluestone Road. There she shows her love to her children freely and enjoys the right to be a mother without restriction. Sethe "had had twenty-eight days—the travel of one whole moon—of enslaved life ... Days of healing, ease, and real-talk, Days of company..." (*Beloved*, 95). In addition, during her stay in 124 House, her mother-in-law, Baby Suggs, and others in the black community help her to overcome the physical and psychological trauma. However, Schoolteacher, the slave owner, comes to capture Sethe and her children. His coming destroys her dream of freedom. Sethe does not know how to protect her children, and finally determines to kill her children and then commit suicide. Sethe insists that she kills her daughter simply out of love, out of her unwillingness to see that her dear children will be captured as slaves like herself. Infanticide is the only way for her to save her children from slavery. Morrison states that, as a desperate slave mother, Sethe has nothing to do:

> And if she thought anything, it was no. no. no, no simple, then she just flew. Collected every bit of her life she had made, all the parts of her that were precious and fine and beautiful, and carried, pushed, dragged them through the veil, out, away, over there where no one could hurt them. Over there, outside this place, where they could be safe. (163)

It shows the immorality of infanticide is attributable to the cruelty of system slavery rather than the mother herself. Since Sethe has experienced the tragic life as a slave mother, she could not let her children experience the same suffering as her:

> And though she and the others lived through and got over it, she could never let it happen to her own. The best thing she has was her children. Whites might dirty her all right. But not her best thing, her beautiful, magical thing—the part of her that was clean. (251)

To Sethe, children are the most precious and best thing she has. It is her deep maternal love that encourages her to overcome all those unbearable troubles and kill her crawling daughter to prevent her from being a slave. Just as Zhu Xiaolin explains that "the black mother who kills her children are those with the lowest social status. To them, violence sometimes is a kind of means to protect her family" (Zhu, 2008:17). With this inhumane way, Sethe succeeds in keeping them from the life of being slaves, although she pays a great price for that. In the following eighteen years, Sethe lives in endless remorse for her baby girl. She is misunderstood, condemned by the community, haunted by the dead baby ghost, and obsessed in the pain of the past. However, she never regrets what she has done. She thinks that infanticide is "the perfect death of her crawling-already baby" (99). What Sethe strives for is the right to protect and love her children which have been deprived and distorted by slavery. She wants to regain her maternal right and claims them as her own. Just as Elizabeth Fox-Genovese explains that because children are the "master's property", some slave women feel that "by killing an infant they loved, they would be in some way reclaiming it as her own" (Fox-Genovese, 1998: 324). So Sethe's infanticide reflects her determination to achieve motherhood with violence. She realizes that as a slave mother, her children would be taken away and never belong to herself. So she chooses violence as her weapon to defend her maternal love. Sethe's infanticide prevents her children from the tragic fate of being slaves. But as to the moral questions of right or wrong of her infanticide, Morrison explains in an interview as follows:

> Under those theatrical circumstances of slavery, if you made that claim, an unheard-of claim, which is that you are the mother of these children that's an outrageous claim for a slave woman. She just became a mother, which is becoming a human being in a situation which is earnestly dependent on your not being one that's who she is. So to claim responsibility for children, to say something about what happens to them mean that you claim all of it, not part of it. Therefore when she is away from her husband, she merges into that role, and it's unleashed and it is fierce. She almost steps over into what she was terrified of being regarded as, which is an animal. It's an excess of maternal feeling, a total surrender to the commitment, and, you know, such excesses are not good. She has stepped across the line, so to speak. It is understandable but is excessive. This is what the townspeople in Cincinnati respond to, not her grief, but her arrogance. (Taylor-Guthrie, 1994: 252)

In Morrison's view, Sethe's infanticide is caused by her maternal love under the cruelty of slavery, which is understandable. Obsessed with the possessive maternal love for her children, when her "best thing" is threatened by Schoolteacher, Sethe takes no hesitation to kill them rather than have them dirtied and destroyed by the slave owner. Her abnormal action is the result of an abnormal society. Eusebio L. Rodrigues says:

> Mother love, when not allowed free expression and growth in human society, remains a primal instinct. Fiercely possessive and predatory, it kills to protect the young from the enemy. (Rodrigues, 1991: 160)

It is the institution of slavery that should take responsibility for the distortion of maternal love. Through Sethe's infanticide, Morrison presents the violent motherhood under the slavery system.

Like Pauline in *The Bluest Eye*, Sweetness, as a mother in *God Help the Child*, fails to take the responsibility of nurturing, protecting, and educating her daughter. Following her grandmother and mother's footsteps, Sweetness is assimilated with the white-dominant culture. When Bride is born, Sweetness is disgusted because her daughter is "Midnight black, Sudanese black" (*God Help the Child*, 3). Sweetness takes Bride as an embarrassment to her and her husband. She even tries to end her life with a blanket over her face or send her to an orphanage someplace. Although Sweetness does not abandon Bride, she treats her daughter coldly and ruthlessly. She is extremely strict to her daughter, "I had to be strict, very strict. Bride needed to learn how to behave, how to keep her head down, and not to make trouble" (7). Scorning of Bride's black skin, Sweetness even abandons her responsibility of nurturing. She says, "Nursing her was like having a pick ninny sucking my teat." (5) So she chooses bottle feeding instead of breastfeeding. She refuses to have any intimate physical contact with Bride, and even when Bride makes a mistake, Sweetness chooses to punish her with a broom rather than with hands. For Bride, she always longs for the touch of her mother, "I used to pray that she would slap my face or spank me just to feel her touch" (31). Bride is so eager for her mother's love that sometimes she even makes some mistakes deliberately to get her mother's attention. She is always afraid of being neglected and blamed by her mother. What is worse, feeling ashamed of Bride's black skin, Sweetness even asks her to call herself "Sweetness" instead of "Mother" or "Mama".

Mother accompanies the children most of the time and influences children's views on family and society. As Giddens (1991: 119) says, "In one family, the relationship between mother and child is most important because the mother plays a crucial role in the whole life of the child." And Erich Fromm claims that "motherly love is an unconditional affirmation of the child's life and his needs" (Fromm, 2006: 45). Here the affirmation consists of two aspects: one is motherly care and responsibility which guarantee the child's growing-up; the other is to cultivate the child with a positive attitude towards life. As a mother, Sweetness indeed raises her daughter to be a grown-up, but she completely fails her responsibility of educating her child. According to Morrison, the responsibilities of mother's work "in terms of four distinct yet interrelated tasks; namely, preservation, nurturance, cultural bearing, and healing" (O'Reilly, 2004:26), it means that mothers should protect their children and teach them to be an upright person. However, when Bride happens to see the landlord Mr. Leigh's disgusting obscenity with a little white boy, her mother asks her to keep her mouth shut for fear of being driven out by the landlord. And at last, an innocent teacher is accused of obscenity and put into prison for fifteen years, which haunts Bride for the rest of her life with remorse. Confucianism puts up with the concept of "enlightening the ignorant and making them follow the right path" (*mengyi yangzheng*, 蒙以养正) which means that the ignorant person should be enlightened through education so that they could follow the right path. This education must begin from early childhood when parents act as the first teacher to children's growth. It stresses the importance of education from parents. Sweetness's immoral guidance of Bride not only harms but also causes severe psychological trauma to her daughter.

Having discussed paternal love and maternal love for children, it is clear that parents should bear the responsibility to raise and educate their children with love and upright values. So far, this section has focuses on parents' responsibility to children, and the final part of this section moves on to discuss children's obligation to their parents.

3.1.3 Filial Piety of Children

Confucian "unity of Heaven and human" claims that to achieve humanity at large, one should love one's parents first and then extend love to others in family and society. Just as Confucius puts forward:

> Those who called filial today are considered so because they can provide for their parents. But even dogs and horses are given that much care. If you do not respect your parents, what is the difference? (Annping, 2014: 34)

Children should love, respect, and care about their parents, which is the basic characteristic of being a human being. As for Morrison, children's obligation to their parents in parents-children relationship is also one of her major concerns. By describing some characters' self-destruction caused by their disrespectful and rebellious behaviors towards parents, Morrison indicates that one must conduct filial piety to their parents to become a person with a complete identity. In this section, the author adopts two characters, Solomon from *Song of Solomon* and Jadine Childs from *Tar Baby* to explore children's filial piety towards parents.

According to Confucianism, the first aspect of filial piety is that children should love, respect, and care for their parents. In *Song of Solomon*, Solomon's parents' relationship is tense and full of conflict. Solomon never tries to help them to clear the misunderstanding. When his father tells him about his mother's incestuous love for his grandfather, Milkman responds with indifference:

As though a stranger that he'd sat next to on a park bench had turned toward him and begun to relate some intimacy ... he himself was not involved or in any way threatened by the stranger's story. (*Solomon*, 74–75)

As for his mother, Morrison never "thought of his mother as a person, a separate individual, with a life apart from allowing or interfering with his own" (75). He is totally indifferent towards his mother. When his mother tells Solomon how cruel and ruthless his father is, Milkman shows no sympathy to his mother and just wants to run away from his parents and family:

I just know that I want to live my own life ... My family's driving me crazy. Daddy wants me to be like him and hate my mother. My mother wants me to think like her and hate my father. Corinthians won't speak to me; Lena wants me out. (221)

Milkman is too selfish to care for others, even his parents. When they need him, he can not understand and support them as they expected. What is worse, when his father beats his mother in a quarrel, Milkman knocks his father down:

Before his father could draw his hand back, Milkman had yanked him by the back of his coat collar, up out of his chair, and knocked him into the radiator the window shade flapped and rolled itself up. "You touch her again, one more time, and I'll kill you." (53)

Milkman is afraid of his father when he is young. However, when he grows up, he starts to show his rebellion. He does everything that his father does not want him to do and rebels with his father as much as he dares:

Macon was clean-shaven; Milkman was desperate for a mustache.

Macon wore bow ties; Milkman wore four-in-hands. Macon didn't part his hair; Milkman had a part shaved into his. Macon hated tobacco; Milkman tried to put a cigarette in his mouth every fifteen minutes. Macon hoarded his money; Milkman gave his away. (63)

He tries to rebel against his father with different methods, which leads to an alienated father-son relationship. Milkman does not know what filial piety is. His alienation and indifference to his parents also hinder his spiritual growth into a person of integrity. Confucius claims that filial piety (*xiao*, 孝) is the root of humanity:

A gentleman looks after the roots. With the roots firmly established, a moral way will grow. Is it not true then that being filial to one's parents and being respectful to one's elders are the roots of one's humanity? (Annping, 2014: 34)

Filial piety is the root for a gentleman to cultivate his morality. If a human can't show his love for his parents, it is impossible to become a great man. As the son in the family, Milkman's failure to show filial piety toward his parents is an important reason for his spiritual barrenness.

Jadine Childs in *Tar Baby* is another representative figure depicted by Morrison who ignores the traditional virtue of filial piety to the elders. In "The Fabulous World of Toni Morrison: *Tar Baby*" (2008), Eleanor W. Traylor studies the relationship between Jadine and Son Green. It focuses on Jadine's internalization with the white culture and Son's persistence of connecting with the black culture, which is of great significance to study. This book is interested in examining Jadine's relationship with her uncle and aunt, who act as parents to raise her up.

Jadine is a fashionable, beautiful, and highly-educated bourgeoisie African American woman. She is also a sophisticated art historian, high-fashion model, and part-time actress. When Jadine is a child, her parents pass away and she takes refuge in her uncle and aunt's place:

> They educated me, and paid for my travel, my lodgings, my clothes, my schools. My mother died when I was twelve; my father when I was two. I'm an orphan. Sydney and Ondine are all the family I have. (*Tar Baby*, 119)

Sydney and Ondine regard Jadine as their own child and sacrifice everything they have for Jadine. Even Ondine's feet hurt too much, she insists on working to earn money to support Jadine, just as Ondine says:

> We don't have a place of our own. And the little bit of savings went to Jadine. Not that I regret a penny of it; I don't. I never minded not having children after we started taking care of her. I would have stood on my feet all day all night to put her through that school. And when my feet were gone, I would have cooked on my knees. (193)

With her uncle and aunt's selfless and unconditional love, Jadine graduates from the famous Sorbonne University in Paris with a degree in art history. She becomes a supermodel on the covers of the famous magazine *Vogue* and *Elle*. Jadine is successful and should be grateful for her uncle and aunt. However, instead of being filial and grateful, Jadine regards herself as superior to her uncle and aunt and takes their love for granted. She does not live with her aunt and uncle; instead, she lives upstairs, symbolizing her superiority over them.

Though Jadine is not a member of the white family, she deems herself as one of them. Jadine thinks that she has received a high-level education and has become a member of the elite, and she does not belong to her uncle's class status anymore. She dines with the Streets family and waits to be served by her uncle. Her uncle serves her at the table "as perfect as he was when he served Mr. Street's friends", but "Jadine did not look at her uncle" (283). Ondine complains about Jadine's behavior, "It didn't use to be this way. Seem like folks used to take care of folks once upon a time. Old black people must be a worrisome thing to the young ones these days." (285) With dignity and superiority over her uncle and aunt, Jadine shows disrespect to them without gratitude. As a daughter, Jadine should take the responsibility of looking after her uncle and aunt, who are like her parents. But when the time comes for Jadine to return her love to her nurturers, she regards them as a burden. And after Jadine returns to New York without considering her uncle and aunt, Son scolds her unfilially behavior:

> They are the ones, who put you through school, woman, they are the ones. Not him. They worked for him all their lives. And you left them down there with him not knowing if they had a job or not. (265)

Jadine attributes her education and success only to Valerine, the white owner, rather than her uncle and aunt. She has completely lost her sense of filial piety even though Ondine treats Jadine as her own daughter without asking for return. At the end of the novel, when Jadine returns to the island to retreat her seal coat, Ondine tells her:

> Jadine, a girl has got to be a daughter first. She has to learn that. And if she never learns how to be a daughter, she can't ever learn how to be woman. I mean a real woman: a woman good enough for a child; good enough for a man—good enough even for the respect of other women. Now you didn't have a mother long enough to learn much about it and I thought I was doing right by sending you to all those schools and so I never told you it and I should have. You don't need your own natural mother to be a daughter. All you need is to feel a certain way, a certain careful way about people older than you are. (283)

However, she replies to her aunt, "You are asking me to parent you. Please don't. I can't do that now." (47) Jadine completely ignores her responsibility of taking care of her adoptive parents, which means her ignorance of the virtue of filial piety. From Ondine's words, it is clear that learning to be a daughter is the first step for a woman to grow into an independent person with self-identity. Filial piety is the fundamental nature for a human to develop and foster other relations with others. Confucian "unity of Heaven and human" insists that people, who cannot show filial piety to his parents, could not have the ability to love other people and be loved by others. Jadine's unfilially behavior leads to her inability of loving herself and other people in her life, foreshadowing her lover, Son's abandonment. Both Morrison and Confucianism attach great importance to children's filial piety towards parents, and human beings need to bear the virtue of filial piety to become a person with a complete identity.

As discussed before, family is the basic unit of society, and the relationship between parents and children is the most important one in a family. In Morrison's novels, the relationship between parents and children is often twisted and alienated. By depicting the absent father and irresponsible mother in the black family, Morrison shows her consciousness on family ethical relationships and emphasizes the importance of building up a harmonious and healthy parent-child relationship. Both Confucianism and Morrison demonstrate the necessity to keep a harmonious relationship between parents and children. Except for familial relations, human beings also have contact with other people and deal with various social relations in life, through which human beings establish their social identity. So far, the relationship between parents and children has been examined, in the following section, the book moves on to discuss the relationship among people in society.

3.2 Social Relationship with Others in Society

Confucian "unity of Heaven and human" insists that everyone lives with various kinds of relationship in society, and deals with these social relations with humanity and morality. In society, people of different races, cultures, and gender should bear the morality of benevolence (*ren*, 仁) toward other people. To analyze the character " 仁 " from the etymological perspective, this character consists of " 人 " and " 二 ". " 人 " means human, and " 二 " means two. According to Ames and Rosemont, the character "underscores the Confucian assumption that one cannot become a person by oneself, and we are, from our inchoate beginnings, irreducibly social" (Ames & Rosemont, 1998: 48). A person lives with all kinds of interpersonal relations with others in society. Moreover, " 仁 " in the "unity of Heaven and human" reflects the mutual respect and love among people. Just as Mencius states in *Mencius*, "He who is benevolent loves others, and he who has manners respects others. He who loves others is loved by others and he who respects others is respected by others." Confucianism attaches great importance to the interpersonal relationship between people.

Morrison claims that it is necessary to establish stable relationships with others to seek support and strength to construct one's self-identity in society. Nobody is able to live isolated in society and needs to have interaction with others, which exactly corresponds to the idea of "unity of Heaven and human". This part analyzes the distorted social relationships among people that hinder characters' self-growth. It also examines characters' process of reconstructing self-identity by reestablishing relations with others in society. Morrison shows the importance of keeping stable relations with other people in society. Let us now turn to the distorted social relations in Morrison's three novels, *Sula*, *Paradise*, and *Song of Solomon*.

3.2.1 Distorted Social Relations

Confucian "unity of Heaven and human" holds that the premise of being loved and respected by others is to love and respect others first. People should take benevolence as the basic moral principle to treat other people to establish a harmonious society. Benevolence is manifested in the affection one has for his family members, as well as compassion for the suffering of other people, and even concern for non-human animals and plants. Confucianism believes that a fully benevolent person will be disposed to recognize the suffering of others and to act appropriately towards others. Morrison has an acute observation of the life of African Americans. She describes different kinds of deformed relationships in society, includes the relationship between white Americans and black Americans, among black Americans, and between individual and community. By exploring these relations in her works, Morrison aims to call for the elimination of different kinds of discrimination between people, and to establish harmonious social relations advocated by Confucianism.

The first aspect of deformed social relations is between white Americans and black Americans. In an interview, Morrison shows her attitude about the inequality between them:

> Black people, because of their physical difference they could be seen as slaves, subsequently are viewed as the visible poor now. We are perceived as the lowest of the classes because we can be identified in that way. It wouldn't make any difference what we wore, or what neighborhood we lived in, we're still visible like that. The visibility has made the prejudices last longer. It's not because one is black that the prejudice exists. The prejudice exists because one can identify the person who was once a slave or in the lower class, and the caste system can survive longer. (Ruas, 1985: 141)

Morrison's investigation is not limited to present the discrimination of white Americans against black Americans. She tries to show the unequal racial relationship between them. Living in a society with racial and cultural discrimination, black Americans suffer dramatically physical and psychological trauma. They want to integrate into the white society; however, they are deprived of basic human rights and are always marginalized in society. In addition, because they are far from their ancestral homeland and cultures, they lack a sense of belonging and cultural identities. In this part, the author adopts Morrison's *Sula*, *Paradise,* and *Song of Solomon* to demonstrate the distorted social relations existing in society.

In *Sula*, there is a black neighborhood named Bottom in the town of Medallion, which is located high in the mountain. Morrison uses the term Bottom with an ironic meaning. It stands for the lower social status of African Americans in the white-dominated society. Bottom shows that white people occupy the fertile land while black Americans are forced to live in the barren land high up in the mountain, "where planting was backbreaking, where the soil slid down and washed away the seeds, and where the wind lingered all through the winter" (*Sula*, 5). They work hard to plant the sterile land with their diligence and have transformed the Bottom into a lovely neighborhood where they live from generation to generation. However, no matter how hard they try, they can't change their miserable situation of being oppressed and discriminated against by the white-dominated society.

Morrison describes the rough lives of African Americans in this novel. War has caused great trauma to human beings, especially to African Americans. Returning from the battlefield, Shadrack is both physically and psychologically injured. The war leaves him nothing, and only "$217 in cash, a full suit of clothes and copies of very official-looking papers" (10) is all his possession. Though he has risked his life on the battlefield, he can't get the same treatment and honor as the white soldiers. He is arrested by the police when he is wandering in the white neighborhood, "They took him to jail, booked him or vagrancy and intoxication, and locked him in a cell" (13). The war has destroyed his mental health, and he suffers a sense of spiritual loss. The cruelty and inequality of the society trigger Shadrack's hatred towards the white people, which is also the reason why he creates the National Suicide Day. The idea of National Suicide Day is "if one day a year were devoted to it, everybody could get it out of the way and the rest of the year would be safe and free" (14). This day offers him a way to get a sense of security and existence. From Shadrack's experience, we see that African American soldiers devote their lives to the war but are abandoned by society after the war. They can't obtain the same high rewards and status as the white soldiers and only live with the painful memories of battlefield and unspeakable trauma.

Another example is Jude, a handsome African American man, who is dissatisfied with being a waiter at the Hotel Medallion. When he knows the town is building a new road, Jude applies for the job "not just for the good money, more for the work itself". He dreams to get the job and proves his value in the community:

> Got that building the New Road, to bring honor to the black community. However, after six days of waiting, he realizes that only the white men even some are much older and weaker are employed. He is only refused by "Nothing else today. Come back tomorrow". (82)

However, he is rejected only because he is an African American. Denied and insulted by the white mainstream society, Jude feels shameful and angry as an African American and gradually loses his self-identity. He becomes a coward and fears to take responsibility for his family. As Morrison depicts in the novel, he runs away from home and abandons his wife and children after he has affairs with Sula. The discrimination of the white towards African Americans not only deprives their right of living a better life but also destroys their confidence of being a husband and a father.

In the novel, black women have been subjected to political, cultural, and economic inferiority in a white-dominated society. Helene is a respected woman in the black community, who "won all social battles with presence and a conviction of the legitimacy of her authority" (18). However, on the way to see her aunt, Helene and Nel are insulted by the white people, which destroys Helene's dignity and self-esteem. It is a mistake that they enter the wrong coach, which is only for the white to sit. African Americans are forbidden to share the same coach with the whites but must go to the "COLORED ONLY" ones. And if they take the wrong coach, they are met with embarrassment and condemnation, as the conductor says, "What you thinking you doin', gal" (20). Later, during the journey, African Americans are permitted only to use colored toilets. Their pride and dignity have been completely ruined and broken down by the white people.

From all the descriptions of the rough living conditions of African Americans, Morison shows the cruelty and ruthlessness of racial discrimination, and describes the great pain they suffer from under the unequal social structure. In the following part, the author moves on to examine the deformed social relationships among African Americans.

Racial discrimination and oppression cause serious damage to the physical and mental health of African Americans. The whites' patriarchal world outlook not only destroys the black race but also distorts its value system, which causes division and conflict between them. In her works, Morrison examines the discrimination between African Americans, including discrimination from the light-skinned blacks towards the dark-skinned blacks; from the middle-class blacks to the poor blacks, and from the dark-skinned blacks to the light-skinned ones. At the end of the 19th century, a large number of black people migrate from the south to the northern cities to seek a better life. After years of hard-working, some of the light-skinned blacks have become middle-class members and gained a sense of superiority over the dark-skinned poor blacks. They are internalized with the whites' aesthetic standard and start to exert the same discrimination against dark-skinned ones. What is worse, they distinguish themselves from the underprivileged African Americans and treat them arrogantly as "Other". The original mutual-love and close-connection between black people are decreased. In the black traditional culture, the black community is regarded as a spiritual home that provides consolation and strength for African Americans to live. However, now it becomes a place with a similar discrimination between them.

The conflicts between African Americans are evident in *Paradise*. The first sentence of this novel is that "they shoot the white girl first" (*Paradise*, 1), which shows that racism is a serious topic throughout the whole story. African Americans' hostile attitude towards the white is described vividly in this sentence. Ruby is an excluded black community isolated from the outside world to escape from the oppression of the white people. Such isolation and exclusion take effect at the beginning. However, after several years, the black community begins to fall apart from the inside:

> The collapse of Ruby does not lie in the intrusion from the whites or the Convent, but from people's incompatible conflicts within their community, by reversing the racism they used to suffer from and making it a new tournament to those light-skinned people, which is a clumsy imitation of the society they have escaped. (Hilfrich, 2006: 331)

People in Ruby regard the dark-skinned blacks as superior because their personality is as pure as their blood. Those light-skinned blacks are inferior to them because they are descendants of the white people in the past. For fear of contaminating the purity of blood, they begin intermarriage between holy families of dark-skinned ones. According to this rule, dark-skinned blacks are not allowed to marry light-skinned ones. Roger Best, an original resident of Ruby Town, is the first to violate the blood rule. He is treated brutally by his town fellows for he marries a light-skinned black woman. Coming to Oklahoma after many hardships, Roger's grandfather makes a great contribution to the foundation and prosperity of Ruby. However, because Roger marries a light-skinned black girl, his grandfather's name is deleted from the list of nine founding fathers of the town and is treated like "the one nobody admitted existed" (195). Roger has to do the lowest and hardest job in Ruby and is completely alienated by other people. No one wants to talk to him and nobody helps him. When his wife has a hard time delivering, other people especially the men, refuse to offer help, and leads to the death of his wife and unborn baby. Roger's family is despised by other African Americans in the town. Deacon and Steward, the bankers in the town, turn down his application for a loan to start his business, and he has to find a job outside of the town.

Roger's daughter Patricia and his granddaughter Billie are also treated badly by other African Americans in Ruby. His daughter, Patricia marries one of the dark-skinned people in the town against her own will, hoping that her children could be dark-skinned to gain fair treatment from other people. However, her daughter is a light-skinned girl just like her. Her husband dies early, which makes her miserable life get worse. When Patricia begins to write a collection of family trees in Ruby to please townspeople, she realizes that other people despise her because of her skin color rather than her personality. She tells her father the brutal reality:

> Daddy, they don't hate us because Mama was your first customer. They hate us because she looked like a cracker and was bound to have cracker-looking children like me. Well, you can see the problems with blood rules. (196)

What's more, other African Americans speak ill of her daughter, Billie, calling her a loose girl even she is only two years old. Billie is deemed as a profligate woman while she is still a virgin. However, when Arnett Fleetwood, the "racially pure" daughter of Jeff Fleetwood, has had sex with K.D. at the age of fourteen, the whole town supports her just because she is a dark-skinned girl. "Skin color trumps morality and becomes the only criterion to judge people in Ruby." (Zhao, 2011:157) In this black community, people tend to judge others by their skin color, rather than by their inner virtue. People's vicious words make Patricia become a strict and bitter mother. She always beats Billie because her daughter has the same skin color as her. Her strictness greatly harms the mother-daughter relationship.

In conclusion, just like the evil of discrimination from the white people, the confrontation and conflicts between African Americans also have a vicious effect on their lives. If they are reluctant to change the patriarchal dominance on others and abort the skin color judgment standard, the town is collapsed without doubt, just as the preacher Misner says:

> Finally, they think they have outfoxed the Whiteman when in fact they imitate him. They think they are protecting their wives and children, when in fact they are maiming them. And when the maimed children ask for help, they look elsewhere for the cause ... Unbridled by Scripture, deafened by the roar of its own history, Ruby was an unnecessary failure. (306)

Morrison detects the problems within the black race, such as extreme arrogance, immobility, and male hegemony, etc., which are harmful to the development and harmony of the black race. Speaking about *Paradise*, Morrison believes that they construct an isolated and patriarchal society in Ruby by the doctrines of Christianity, as it is a unique and isolated paradise with all its townspeople are African Americans. Morrison said in an interview:

> The isolation, the separateness, is always a part of any utopia. And it was my mediation if you will, and interrogation of the whole idea of paradise,

the safe place, the place full of bounty, where no one can harm you. But, in addition to that, it's based on the notion of exclusivity. (310)

Moreover, Morrison states that she "wanted to force the reader to become acquainted with the communities" and to replicate the experience of "walk[ing] into a neighborhood".

Confucian "unity between Heaven and human" holds that an individual can't live isolated from other people in society, and everyone interacts with other people to construct his identity. An individual needs to maintain a harmonious relationship with people in society in order to achieve his own life meaning and gain a spiritual growth so as to become an authentic human being. However, the discrimination from the whites and the conflict between the fellow black people lead to their loneliness and isolation. In *Song of Solomon*, for Macon and Milkman, loneliness is their state of existence. Both suffer from external and internal loneliness because of their disconnected relationship with other people in society.

Macon Dead is a middle-class African American man who has achieved success in wealth. However, he lives a pathetic and lonely life without any pleasure and meaning. His loneliness and alienated relationship with other people results from his money-oriented value influenced by capitalism as well as his ruthlessness toward other people. The object of his life is to accumulate wealth in extreme ways without showing mercy to people around him. People in the community all hate and despise Macon's family because his ruthlessness. For example, Porter is one of his tenants, when he gets drunk, he points at Macon and says, "You the worst. You need killing. You need killing. You know why?" "Everybody knows why." (*Solomon*, 26) At last, Macon asks the janitor Freddie to get the money from Porter's pocket when he falls asleep after he's passed out. Macon is rejected by other people in the black community. Meanwhile, he is looked down upon by the white people. He lives a life with an alienated relationship with both black Americans and white Americans, which leads to his lonely and unhappy life.

Under the influence of his father, Milkman inherits the value of materialism and has the sense of superiority over other poor blacks. He is obsessed with money and property just like his father. He is alienated from his family as well as other people in the community. When he is a child, at school, both the white children and the black children make fun of him and do not play with him:

> As soon as he got up off the knees at the window sill, grieving because he could not fly, and went off to school, his velvet suit separated him from the other children. White and black thought he was a riot and went out their way to laugh at him and see to it that he had no lunch to eat or any crayons, nor even go through the line to the toilet or the water fountain. (264)

When he grows up, at the age of thirteen, Milkman is disdained by other African Americans when he helps his father with the rent collection. Once, he goes to the bar with Guitar, the black fellows refuse to let him in because he is from the Dead's family. He receives rejection and condemnation from the black community until his adolescence. He does not do anything to change this situation but show an indifferent attitude to everything and everybody in his life. He becomes an outsider disconnected from other people. What is more, he feels bored with everything such as money, politics, and city, "his life was pointless, aimless" (107).

Because of his indifference, he shows a cold attitude to the death of the African American boy Emmette Till. When he hears Till is stomped to death in Sunflower County, he does not care about the boy's death but saying "fuck Till, I am the one in trouble" (88). Milkman's ruthlessness and indifference to other blacks are one of the reasons why he is alienated from other people in the community. When Milkman arrives at Shalimar, he is also rejected by other

African Americans because of his arrogance, "Nobody came toward him, and offered his a cigarette or a glass of water. Only the children and the hens walked around. Under the hot sun, Milkman was frozen with anger" (199). In the north, "His name spelled deadly and grudging respect. But here, in the south, he was unknown, unloved, and damn near killed" (200). The reason why people in the south hate him is that Milkman is so arrogant and indifferent because he has assimilated into the white culture. He cares only about himself and exerts superiority over other people. He has become an immature and aimless person with an alienated and disharmonious relationship with others.

Milkman's failure to establish a harmonious relationship with others in the community leads to his spiritual incompleteness which hinders him to become a human with self-identity. In Morrison's works, African Americans are always trapped in the contradictions between the white and the black culture. They lead a confused and aimless life and alienated from the whole society. At the same time, there is some discrimination among African Americans themselves. As Hu Jun (2007: 47) states, "It is poverty that makes the blacks stand together, and the black middle class passes the frustration they encounter in the white world to the poor blacks, and exploit the lower class." This section has examined the disharmonious relationship between people in Morrison's novels, mainly focusing on the conflict and discrimination between white Americans and black Americans, as well as among black Americans in the community. In contrast to this, the following section examines the significance of constructing harmonious social relations for people in society in Morrison's works.

3.2.2 Construction of Harmonious Social Relations

Confucian "unity of Heaven and human" advocates that it is impossible for a human to live without social relationships, Morrison also shows a deep concern for different social relations among human beings. As examined in the previous part, the deformed and disharmonious relationship between people are examined from three aspects, including the intraracial discrimination between white Americans and black Americans, interracial oppression among black Americans, and individual's alienation from the black community. All these factors lead to black Americans' incomplete sense of subjectivity. In order to establish self-identity, it is essential for human beings to construct stable and harmonious social relations. In this part, the author demonstrates the importance of harmonious relationships between people of different races, people of the same race, and an individual with the community. All these are essential in human's self-growth and achievements. The author examines the relationship in Morrison's *Song of Solomon*, *Home*, and *Beloved*. Though all of Morrison's novels touching this topic, these three novels display it more evidently.

In *Song of Solomon*, Milkman's journey into the south is a quest for knowledge of his family and ancestral history. Finally, he finds his family roots and reconnects with the black community. Many critics have studied Milkman's quest for his true self with the help of the community. For example, Theodore O. Mason, Jr.'s essay "The Novelist as Conservators: Stories and Comprehension in Toni Morrison's *Song of Solomon*" (1988), studies how Milkman acquires his true self after understanding family history and being able to distinguish authentic from inauthentic stories held by people around him in the community. In "Folklore and Community in *Song of Solomon*" (1980), Susan L. Blake explores what Morrison means by the community through studying how the writer appropriates the folklore of flying Africans in *Song of Solomon*. In addition, Valerie Smith's "The Quest for and Discovery of Identity in Toni Morrison's *Song of Solomon*" (1985) argues Milkman discovers his identity after his journey to the south which turns out to be spiritual rather than material. The author totally agrees with the critics' idea of the connection between Solomon and the community. Moreover, this book focuses on Milkman's construction of social relations which function as the basis for his realization of self-identity.

At the age of thirty, Milkman's life is still aimless and in a mess. Under the influence of his materialistic father, Milkman is ruthless and indifferent towards the people around him. He has alienated from his family as well as the black community. And he is ignorant of the history of his ancestors and family, and losses connection with the black people and the black culture. In order to escape from his father's control and the deformed family, he decides to head for the south to search for gold. The journey introduces several teachers and helpers to Milkman, bringing him closer to his family history and ancestors. His first teacher is Circe, who witnesses the murder of Milkman's grandfather by white men. Circe tells Milkman about the white oppression of the black slaves and the story of his grandmother, which makes Milkman start to think about his black identity for the first time. Milkman also gets his real family name from Circe, which helps him regain his family root and black identity. He learns that it is his responsibility to keep and preserve his family name and pass it down to the next generation.

After his encounter with Circe in Denville, Milkman meets the priest Reverend Cooper, who tells him the evils of white Americans to black Americans. Milkman starts to question why they do not take action to change their oppressed life. He realizes that as a descendant of Africans, he should fight against the whites and bond together with other black Americans. Afterward, Milkman arrives at Shalimar where his grandfather lives. Different from the north, the black people in Shalimar are closely connected. This place makes him get closer to his family's past and African culture. He hears more about the flying story of his great-grandfather Jake Solomon and his great-grandmother Ryna from the local community. He is eager to seek the family's origins and history. While hunting with fellow black people, Milkman goes through a trail of death, realizing that money, property, and material accumulation mean nothing to him in front of the natural world, "There was nothing to help him—not his money, his car, his father's reputation, his suit, or shoes ... all he had started with on his journey was gone..." (277). Milkman continues his journey to seek his family history, during which he throws away his clothes, watch, and shoes. He gradually discards the values of the white culture and constructs his cultural identity. As Valeria Smith argues:

> The ultimate sigh of his achievement of identity is his ability to take flight in the way his grandfather did. Milkman bursts the bonds of the Western, individualistic conception of self, accepting its place the richness and complexity of a collective sense of identity. (Smith, 2003: 40)

Milkman starts to realize his selfishness and irresponsibility towards other people around him. He achieves his spiritual growth from a selfish, irresponsible infant to a mature, responsible adult with the help from other people in society. Through his quest for gold in the south, he has constructed a series of relations with other black Americans in the community. Milkman has changed from a man who is psychologically alienated and fragmented to a truly liberated and whole person. Confucian "unity of Heaven and human" also examines the relationship between individual and community. It advocates maintaining a harmonious relationship between the two because they are interdependent and jointly promote each other's development. Moreover, it proposes that individuals should hold a communitarian notion, without which his actions are likely to result in excessive individualism and cause damage to the community. It asks everyone in the community to love and care for others to construct a reliable community. Morrison emphasizes that self-reliance should be realized in the black community instead of alienating oneself from others. What she emphasizes is that subjectivity should be found in the context of community. Paule Marshall says that African Americans have "the ability to recognize one's continuity with the larger community" (Marshall, 1984:159). They have attached much importance to collective survival in the racist society to seek support and love from their community. Morrison shows that those suffered and traumatized African Americans would recover from the past traumas when they gain strength and support from the community. Just as Mbalia (1991: 90) states, "The struggle continues, and solidarity of the black people is their only way to survive, develop and prevail." In the community, people take care of each other. The community is vital in an individual's trauma recovery and self-identity construction. Morrison holds that community is the spiritual home for them. They can get mutual support and love from other people in the community and find their value of living.

Morrison is famous for describing female protagonists who are traumatized and oppressed in the discriminated world in her novels. Different from the depressing theme in her previous novels, *Home* conveys a hopeful, positive, and optimistic future for African Americans. Critics such as Irene Visser, in his essay "Entanglements of Trauma: Relationality and Toni Morrison's *Home*" (2014), shows that relationality presents a method of reading Morrison's *Home* that allows the full scope to the many ways in which Morrison addresses, absorbs, and transforms pre-existing discourses on trauma. Moreover, in "Nature of Racism and Oppression: A Study of Toni Morrison's *Home* and *A Mercy*", Anto Mathias examines the traumatic experiences of the black community. It also describes how every character has a problem dealing with racism. Mathias discusses the trauma of the black community and every character in the novel. In this part, this book focuses on the sisterhood between women, which contributes to their physical and psychological recovery.

Sisterhood, one of Morrison's major themes in her works, refers to feelings of mutual concern and loyalty among women. As Barbara Smith (1978: 21) says, "Morrison points out in her literary works that black women must come together closely just for a living." They get help and strength from other African American women for their own healing. In Morrison's view, women find the other "self" from each other and unite together with sisterhood. They face life, death together, and understand more deeply with each other than their male counterparts. Sisterhood is essential in their lives, especially in process of self-realization and self-identity construction.

In *Home*, sisterhood among African American women not only saves Cee's life but also cures her psychological trauma. Cee arrives at Lotus with severe physical and psychological injures. During her childhood, Lotus is "the worst place in the world" (*Home*, 83), for her evil grandmother, indifferent parents, and the dullness of the town. However, now Lotus has become the place where Cee's trauma is healed with the love from other African American women. She finally constructs her self-identity. When Cee goes back to Lotus, "women took turns nursing Cee and each had a different recipe for her cure" (80). They adopt a series of traditional medical methods with wisdom to cure Cee gradually:

> Cee was different. Two months surrounded by countrywomen who loved mean had changed her. The women handled sickness as though it were an affront, an illegal, invading braggart who needed whipping. (81)

The sisterhood in the community gives Cee the feeling of being loved and empowers her to recover from the wounds. Cee finally heals her physical injures caused by the white doctor and regains a sense of security in the community. From the viewpoint of trauma study, to recover from trauma needs to make a quite safe living environment, and regain a sense of trust, safety, and identity. Within a secure environment, Cee establishes stable relationships with other people and begins to speak out her traumatic experiences.

After Cee's physical recovery, other black women teach her how to be an independent and self-reliant woman. "They brought their embroidery and crocheting, and finally they used Ethel Fordham's house as their quilting center." (83) The period of being cured by other women is the first time Cee has the chance to know about African American women's lives in the community. In Cee's eyes, although their appearances and lifestyles are different, "their similarities were glaring" (123). "They took responsibility for their lives and for whatever, whoever else needed them."(83) Cee learns from other women to be independent and responsible for her own life, and also learns quilting from these women. In the black culture, quilting is sewed by women with pieces of cloth from the used clothes and materials into a new quilt. During the process of quilting, women talk about daily life stories and seek consolation and support from other women. It has become a symbol that black people sew the past and old memories together to make a brand new future. It is a special image bearing the traditional black culture. Cee grasps the skill of quilting to earn money to help the community get electricity. She has become an independent woman with the achievement of independence and self-reliance. What is more, through quilting with other women every day, Cee feels she is one part of the community and no longer isolated in society. Every day she is "surrounded by their comings and goings, listening to their talk, their songs, following their instructions" (124), Cee learns diligence, responsibility, and mutual love from these women. Although they are oppressed by a white-dominated society, they always keep an optimistic and hopeful belief in life.

In Cee's recovery, a typical woman in the community is Ethel, who acts as an instructor and plays the role of mother to Cee. Ethel teaches Cee with confidence and wisdom of life. Cee learns how to do gardening from Ethel and receives her encouragement that "Her garden was not Eden; it was so much more than that" (88). Moreover, Ethel tells Cee that she is the most precious and independent existence in the world and nobody could destroy her identity as a human being:

> See what I mean? Look at yourself. You free. Nothing and nobody is obliged to save you but you. Seed your land. You young and a woman and there's a serious limitation in both, but you a person too. Don't let Lenore or some trifling boyfriend and certainly no devil doctor decide who you are. That's slavery. Somewhere inside you is that free person I'm talking about. Locate her and let her do some good in the world. (85)

Ethel is the spiritual leader of Cee's recovery. As she tells Cee that "nothing and nobody is obliged to save you but you" (126) in the past, Cee depends on other people to give her security and a better life, which causes her great miseries and traumas. With Ethel's love and encouragement, Cee wants "to be the one who rescued her own self" (84), and finally becomes "the person who would never again need rescue" (129). Bit by bit, Cee begins to regain her self-value and get rid of the label of inferiority. The sisterhood love of Miss Ethel and other women in the community not only cures Cee's physical disease but also helps Cee to walk out of her traumatic experiences and love herself. Finally, Cee finds her spiritual home in the community, as she tells Ethel "I ain't going anywhere, Miss Ethel. This is where I belong" (85). Cee's recovery of physical and psychological traumas proves that the sisterhood in the community is essential for an individual to cure the traumas and construct self-identity. Cee succeeds in her pursuit of self-identity after going through serious physical and psychological trauma with the sisterhood love from other women. She tries her best to find the meaning and value of existence and finally constructs her subjectivity as an independent woman. The love and care from other women in the community not only cure Cee's physical trauma but also guide her to the affirmation of self-value and the process of identification.

Similar to Cee's experience, Sethe in *Beloved* also recovers from her traumatic experience by reestablishing a connection with other people in society, especially with sisterhood love from other women. Many critics have studied *Beloved* from the perspective of the community. Such as Bernard W. Bell, in his essay "*Beloved*: A Womanist Neo-Slave Narrative or Multivocal Remembrances of Things Past" (1992), Bell discusses how Sethe's community first turns its back on her and finally comes to their rescue. In "The Ghosts of Slavery: Historical Recovery in Toni Morrison's *Beloved*" (1992), Linda Krumholz gives a detailed description of how the help of neighborhood women becomes a cleansing ritual for Sethe. What's more, in "Narrative and Community Crisis in *Beloved*" (2001),

D' Scott Hinson studies the root of the conflicts within the black community in *Beloved*, contending the community is unable to identify the white oppression as the root of its collapse and entrapment in cycles of violence. And Jennifer Fitzgerald, in her essay "Selfhood and Community: Psychoanalysis and Discourse in *Beloved*" (1993), argues that *Beloved* is concerned with characters trying to acquire subjectivity. It explores not only the psychic damage of slavery also its therapeutic alternative, the supportive community. The essays above all touch on the theme of community and sisterhood between women. In this part, the author gives a further study of the function of community and sisterhood love in Sethe's physical and psychological recovery and subjectivity construction.

In *Beloved*, Morrison has surpassed the scope of African American women, expanding sisterhood among women of different races. Amy Denver is the only white person who helps Sethe during her runaway to the freedom place— Cincinnati. Amy finds Sethe when she falls down in a forest because of exhaustion. Here in the novel, Morrison shades some light on the relationship between white American and black American women. Sethe's escape symbolizes the transition from death to resurrection, while Amy helps her finish this transition. Although both of them are females, they are in quite different situations. Amy is an indentured servant who only sells her labor, not her body, and not the tool of reproduction as African American woman, while Sethe is the property of the slave owners without her own identity and freedom.

At the beginning of their meeting, Amy and Sethe seem to distrust each other because of their different skin colors. When Amy asks her name, Sethe even dares not to tell her true name, but says "Lu". Sethe says, "You don't know how they'll jump. Say one thing, and do another." (*Beloved*, 77) This shows that there is a great prejudice of skin color and distrust among people during that time. However, as Sethe communicates with Amy, she comes to know that Amy is not like the other white people she has ever met. Amy is gentle and friendly and does not treat her as a slave. Amy is also a runaway to escape from the white owner.

Sethe gains a sense of sympathy with her, especially when Amy tells about her bitter life as a servant. Amy is beaten by her employer—Mr. Buddy. She also gets some scar as Sethe does on her back. Both of them are orphans. Amy's mother, who was given to Mr. Buddy, seems to have been raped by him. Amy tells Sethe, "Joe Nathan said Mr. Buddy is my daddy, but I don't believe that." (80) Sethe's mother is also raped by the white men too. Because of their similar experience, the two women have sympathy with each other and establish the relationship of sisterhood soon.

Moreover, Amy's help plays an important role in awakening Sethe's consciousness of being a human being. Amy suggests Sethe to enter the nearby house for fear that Sethe is bitten by snakes in the forest. Under her encouragement and company, Sethe begins crawling towards the house:

> She crawled and Amy walked alongside her, and when Sethe needed to rest, Amy stopped too and talked some more about Boston and velvet and good things to eat. The sound of that voice, like a sixteen-year-old boy's, going on and on and on, kept the little antelope quiet and grazing. (34)

Here, the path to the house symbolizes a road leading to freedom, on which a white girl and an African American woman support each other against hardships. When they reach the shield house, Amy starts to massage Sethe's swollen feet for her restoration, "Good for you. The more it hurt better it is. Can't nothing heals without pain, you know" (79). She keeps massaging Sethe's feet "until she cried salt tears" (78). Amy tenders Sethe carefully. "Sethe felt the fingers of those good hands lightly touch her back." (78) All these shows Amy's compassion and love toward Sethe, which means Amy acts as a healer to treat Sethe's physical wound. Her efforts to relieve Sethe's pain are very important for Sethe to gain courage and strength in her delivery of Denver. Just as Peach Linden argues, it is evident that Amy is "one of the two main healers" (Peach,

1998: 103).

Sethe's delivery of Denver is the climax of the formation of sisterhood between them, for that Amy acts as a midwife. She helps Sethe deliver the baby without hesitation and encourages her during the tough process. And that is why Sethe names her baby girl with the name Denver. During the whole process, Amy never despises Sethe because of her black skin. She only takes Sethe as a woman who needs help and tries her utmost to help Sethe. They are bond together because of the baby:

> A patroller passing would have sniggered to see two throw-away people, two lawless outlaws—a slaves and a barefoot white woman with unpinned hair—wrapping a ten-minute-old baby in the rags they wore. (84)

This sentence presents the sisterhood between them, no matter what skin color they have. Before meeting Amy, Sethe has never been treated like a human being. The only roles she has are worker, servant, and slave owner's reproduction machine. So she doesn't trust and even hates the white people. Meanwhile, she despises herself with black skin and loses a sense of self-worth. Amy's tender treatment gives Sethe a feeling of being a person, not the property or animal. For the first time in her life, she realizes that she is a human being deserved to be loved. The sisterhood with Amy gives Sethe's encouragement and determination to strive for her right to be a human being. Sethe discloses her heart to Amy and regards her as a sister, which is the sigh of her recovery from psychological trauma.

What Amy does conforms to the Confucian concept of "harmony but not uniformity" (he er butong, 和而不同). It also revolves around the mutual-respect of difference among people, which means to achieve overall harmonious co-existence based on respecting differences and diversity. Uniformity and harmony are two different attitudes of treating and accommodating social groups. Uniformity means obliterating differences in everything while harmony is to maintain and respect the differences. Allowing different things to complement and supplement each other makes a harmonious whole full of vitality and creativity. From the viewpoint of Confucianism, harmony is different from uniformity. Just like Confucius states, "The gentleman harmonizes (he, 和) without being an echo. The petty man echoes (tong, 同) and does not harmonize." (Annping, 2014: 253) "Universal Harmony" (datong, 大同) refers to the time of peace and prosperity envisioned by Confucian scholars when all the people under Heaven are one family, equal, friendly, and helpful to each other. Confucianism takes universal harmony as the supreme stage of the development of human society. Its main features are all power and wealth belong to the whole of society; all people are equal and live and work in peace and contentment; everyone is cared for by society; everything is used to its fullest and everyone works to his maximum potential:

> When the Great Way prevails, the world belongs to all the people. People of virtue and competence are chosen to govern the country, which honesty and harmony is the way for people to treat each other. People not only love their parents, bring up their children, but also take care of the aged. The middle-aged are able to put their talents and abilities to best use, children are well nurtured, and old widows and widowers, unmarried old people, orphans, childless old people, and the disabled are all provided for.... This is universal harmony. (*Book of Rites*, 2009: 325)

Sethe's action of naming her new-born baby girl with Denver is a symbol of love and sisterhood between them. Denver has become a link to transracial love. Moreover, through the depiction and narration of Amy's help to Sethe, Morrison shows that in society, no matter what skin color the women are, they could unite together by sisterhood to produce a new future and a harmonious world.

In summary, this chapter has analyzed human's social relations with other people. The link between family members especially with parents is the foremost one as parents play an important role in educating and shaping the characteristics of children. Meanwhile, children should be filial piety towards parents, because it is the fundamental morality of being a human. Except for the familial relationship, one also needs to interact with other people in society. Social relations contribute a lot in one's construction of self-identity. From the above mentioned, it is evident that both Confucian "unity of Heaven and human" and Toni Morrison emphasize the importance of establishing a harmonious relationship with other people in family and society. A detailed discussion of the relationship between human and society has been presented in this chapter. In the following chapter, the book moves on to examine the relationship between human with the inner self in Morrison's novels.

4

Relationship Between Human and Self

The previous two chapters have focused on the interrelationship between human and nature, human and society, existing in the external world of human beings. This chapter examines human's inner world, the relationship between human and the inner self. It is the third aspect of Confucian "unity of Heaven and human" which has been pursued by Confucian scholars for thousands of years. As said in *Book of Rites*, one of the most important Confucian classics:

> Only after the heart-mind has been properly settled, the body can be cultivated. The cultivation of the body makes them the regulation of the family possible, which preconditions a good government. A good government, again, is a precondition for the world peace.

This quotation shows the inner self is fundamental to the existence of human beings. It is important for human beings to deal with the relationship with the inner self in a harmonious way. Confucianism believes that human beings need to keep a harmonious relationship with the inner self to obtain a complete self-identity. Self-identity refers to a group of characteristics possessed by an individual in the evaluation of his life experiences. It gives human beings a sense of personal affirmation of individuality and existence. Jacqueline de Weever in her essay explores self-identity as "the struggle to establish identity in a world which does not acknowledge one's existence is sometimes lost" (Weever, 1979: 403). Self-identity is the premise of being a complete human being.

Confucianism proposes that human needs to handle the relationship between spirit and body by restraining desire and behaviors with morality and virtue in society. Some early Pre-Qin Confucian scholars believed that human moral characters were originated from Heaven. Confucian scholars of the Song Dynasty inherited this concept, further making the notion of "characters endowed by Heaven" profound. It means that all people are endowed by Heaven with moral characters. With connection and unification of human nature and the nature of Heaven, the realm of the "unity of Heaven and human" is achieved with morality. Besides, Confucianism attaches great importance to self-love and self-value in self-identity construction. The basic requirements of human beings to reach a harmonious relationship with the inner self with a complete self-identity are morality and virtues as well as the awareness of self-love and self-value.

African Americans are constantly troubled with their identity crisis, which has always been Morrison's major concern in her works. African Americans came to America and lived as slaves for a long time. They were treated as a property of white people and their identity as human beings were ignored. Even now in America, they are discriminated by white people, especially in certain parts of America. In the majority of her novels, "Morrison highlights the importance of identity, the formation of the 'self', and the influence of the environment and society on that development" (Tamilselvi & Prabha, 2016: 80). In the case of Toni Morrison's characters, "the trauma in question is slavery, not [only] as an institution or even an experience, but as a collective memory, a form of remembrance that grounded the identity-formation of a people" (Eyerman, 2001: 1). Morrison not only describes their spiritual barrenness but also explores the ways to achieve self-affirmation and construct their identities. Through her works, Morrison points out the ways to construct self-identity is to possess morality and virtues as a human being. These are the basic standards and social norms, guiding human thoughts and behaviors. Apart from morality and virtues, self-love and self-value are also indispensable to the establishment of authentic self-hood. Some of Morrison's characters live with spiritual barrenness, suffering from an internal crisis of incoherence and instability. Morrison also depicts several characters with a harmonious spiritual world and has established a complete self-identity in life.

We see that both "unity of Heaven and human" and Toni Morrison emphasize the necessity of harmony between human and the inner self in constructing self-identity. And the proper way to achieve this goal is to cultivate morality and virtues, and to possess the awareness of self-love and self-value. This chapter analyzes Morrison's novels from the spiritual world of human beings. To study the relationship between human and the inner self, this book proves that the idea of Confucian "unity of Heaven and human" concerning human's inner self is demonstrated by Morrison in her works.

4.1 Loss of Self-Identity Caused by Disharmonious Relationship with Self

As presented above, a person with a complete inner self knows morality and virtues of life clearly and is able to restrain his behaviors and thoughts to achieve a harmonious relationship with the inner self. On the contrary, a person without morality and virtues inevitably will conduct some behaviors which influence the well-being of others and his self-identity construction. Morrison describes some characters that live without morality and virtues, and eventually fail to establish their self-identity. There are some characters that live with a complete self-identity because of the possession of morality and virtues as well as self-love and self-value. In the first section, the author examines the lack of morality and virtues in three novels from different stages of Morrison's writing *Sula*, *Paradise*, and *A Mercy*. It proves that this theme runs through her writing career.

4.1.1 Lack of Morality and Virtues

Unlike Morrison's other female characters, Sula is a rebellious woman who refuses to conform to the conventional life and devotes her life to pursue her self-identity. Her rebellious image has attracted many critics' attention. For example, Rykerh's essay "Defenses Mechanisms in *Sula* by Toni Morrison" analyzes several examples of defense mechanisms in *Sula*, such as avoidance, reaction formation, and projection. In "No Bottom and No Top: Oppositions in *Sula*" (1997), Maduhu Dubey gives a rather detailed analysis of the relationship between the black community of Bottom and Sula. Moreover, Cedric Gael Bryant, in his essay "The Orderliness of Disorder: Madness and Evil in Toni Morrison's *Sula*" (1990), studies how the black community tries to coexist with the threat posed to its survival by evil and madness, embodied in such figures as Shadrack and Sula. These criticisms mainly discuss the relationship between the black community and Sula as well as Sula's rebellion. This book explores the reason for Sula's rebellious failure—her lack of morality and virtues.

Sula's rebellious personality is formed under the influence of social environment and her family environment. Living in a black community with racial discrimination and oppression from the male power, Sula realizes the miserable suffering of African American women and decides to make a self that belongs to her own. She is also influenced by her grandmother, Eva, who lives on her own without depending on man. Sula decides to establish a new self-centered value with an absolute ego to challenge the conventional life. Morrison once described her as a special person in society:

> According to Morrison, Sula herself is a masculine character in that sense of morality. She will do the kind of things that normally only men can do, which is why she's so special. (Taylor-Guthrie, 1994: 34)

Sula becomes a woman with "no center, no speck around which to grow on" (*Sula*, 119) However, Morrison shows Sula's failure at the end of the novel. The exact reason behind her failure is Sula's lack of morality and virtues as an individual in the black community. For example, when her mother Hannah burns on fire, Sula watches with indifference and curiosity. She has lost the sense of mercy and affection, even towards her mother. Moreover, she is disobedient to her grandmother, Eva. When Eva urges her to marry and have babies, Sula responds coldly, "I don't want to make somebody else. I want to make myself." (92) She even sends Eva to the old folks' home without mercy. It shows she lives a self-centered life with an absolute ego. Because she has no morality and virtues, Sula abandons her family, her boyfriend, even betrays her best friend Nel. She has sex with any man she wants, even with Nel's husband, and then discards them without any excuse. For Sula, sex is a rebellious way to satisfy her self-pleasure without any moral restriction.

In Sula's view, God is dead and the only thing that she trusts is herself. She defies God and even visits the sacred church without her bra. What is worse, when Sula kills Chicken Little, a little boy, by accident on the riverbank, she does not even feel guilty for her mistake. She has become a self-centered woman without any virtues in society, which leads to her isolation and alienation from family members as well as the community. Just like what Morrison said in an interview with Anne Koenen, she called Sula "the one out of sequence" and constructed as follows:

> I thought she had a serious flaw, which led her into a dangerous zone which is not being able to make a connection with other people. Sula's behavior looks inhuman because she has cut herself off from responsibility to anyone other than herself. Sula put her grandmother away. That is considered awful because among black people that never happened. You must take care of each other. That's more unforgivable than anything else she does because it suggests a lack of her sense of community. Critics devoted to the Western heroic tradition—the individual alone and triumphant—see Sula as a survivor. In the black community, she is lost. (Koenen, 1984: 207–208)

Although Sula never ceases to construct her self-identity, she lacks the knowledge of fighting for independence with other people in the community as a whole. Her lonely rebellion only leads to self-destruction and early death. In another interview with Robert Stepto, Morrison offered her critique of Sula:

> [She] knows all there is to know about herself, because she examines herself, she is experimental with herself, she is perfectly willing to think the unthinkable thing. But she has trouble making a connection with other people and just feeling that lovely sense of accomplishment of being close in a very strong way. (Taylor-Guthrie, 1994: 14)

Sula ignores the responsibility as a human being in the community. From the Confucian perspective, all her inappropriate behaviors due to her lack of "righteousness" (*yi*, 义). Righteousness means "reasonable" and "properness", containing two extended meanings. One is the proper basis and standard for people's actions. The other is to adjust one's words or deeds to meet certain standards, under the guidance of moral judgments. Scholars in the Song Dynasty used *li* (理) or "principles of heaven" to interpret *yi* and considered *yi* to be the reasonable standard defined by the "principles of Heaven", and hoped that human's words and deeds would fall in line with the "principles of Heaven". Just like Zhu Xi, the Confucian scholar in the Song Dynasty stated, "Righteousness means exercising self-restraint to do everything properly." (Zhu, 1986: 97) It means that a person with righteousness could control his desires and guide his behaviors properly in life, and could keep a harmonious relationship with others and his self. However, Sula does everything according to her own will without righteousness, which leads to her self-destruction and alienation from other people in the community.

Moreover, Sula's behavior is against the Confucian concept of "rites" (*li*, 礼), which is a general term for social norms that regulate interrelationship between people. By setting various regulations about ceremonies, rituals, and systems, rites define an individual's specific status and corresponding duty and power, thereby differentiating people in the community in terms of age, kinship, and social status. With such a differentiation, the rites determine the proper position of each individual. It is the main factor for human beings to achieve harmony between other people, and everything else in nature. An extended concept from *The Analects* implicates the same meaning with "rites". It is to "restrain oneself and conform to social norms". The term means to restrain one's words and deeds to comply with social norms. It is the fundamental method recommended by Confucius for achieving benevolence. According to Confucius, social norms should be the standard for cultivating benevolence. Externally, one's words and deeds should be subject to social norms, but more importantly, a person should restrain his selfish desires to see, listen, speak, and act within such norms. When one "restrains oneself and practice propriety", he achieves harmony between his body and mind. Although Sula demonstrates herself with all her efforts, trying to define a new black woman image, the way she adopts is beyond morality and against ethical principles, which leads to her self-destructive individualism.

Another significant example is Ruby Town in *Paradise*. Established in 1949, Ruby Town is an exclusively all-black community whose members have been rejected mercilessly by both white Americans and light-skinned blacks for they are too black and too poor. During their journey to the West area, "They don't know we or about we," said one man. "Us free like them; was salve like them. What is this difference?" (*Paradise*, 14) Owning to such a bitter experience of "Disallowing", they choose to alienate themselves from the mainstream society which is full of discrimination. It seems that people in Ruby live a decent and affluent life by selling ranches to gas and railway companies during the rapid development of industrialization. However, they still cannot shake off the shadow brought by internalized colonial memory, which leads to the collapse of their spiritual world.

The most outstanding example is Morgan brothers, who are veterans from the

Second World War. They used to be compassionate and benevolent. As the marginalized ethnic group, the feeling of inferiority is intensified, which results in the imbalance within their minds. What's more, they pursue superiority in Ruby as a compensation for the maltreatment received on the battlefield. After gaining a good economic and social status in Ruby, they regard themselves as the legitimate governors of the whole town. Though they flee from the American mainstream society, they have been deeply trapped in their value system. With the accumulation of power and wealth, their vanity and selfishness increase accordingly. They lose their sympathy, dignity, and humanity and become indifferent to others' sufferings.

Deacon once fell in love with Consolata, however, when he finds his masculinity is offended by her, he abandons her immediately and kills her in the Convent massacre without hesitation. He has become a ruthless person without any affection. What's more, the Morgan brothers refuse to integrate with the white culture for the fear of contaminating the value system within Ruby. When they detect that the Convent women are likely to pose a threat to their masculinity, they take revenge by violence, murdering these unarmed women to prove their power. Their behaviors prove their lack of "considerate" (*shu*, 恕), which has been defined in Confucianism. The basic meaning of "considerate" is to put oneself in another person's position and have empathy. When one behaves like this, he understands and shows considerations for the interests of others. Based on the understanding, people should refrain from imposing their likes and dislike on others. To those who are enforcing the law and who are victims of wrongdoing, the extended meaning of this term is forgiveness or pardon. One of Confucius's disciples named Zigong once asked Confucius:

"Is there a single word that can serve as the guide to conduct throughout one's life?" Confucius replied, "It is perhaps the word *shu*. Do not impose on others what you do not want [others to impose on you]." (Annping, 2014: 302)

Confucius insists that "considerate" is a moral character which is a lifelong pursuit for an exemplary person. Because of their lack of moral character as "considerate", the Morgan brothers become more arrogant and cruel toward other people in the community. As the leader of the Ruby community, the Morgan Brothers do not possess morality and virtues, which at last leads to the tragedy of the Convent women and their own.

The story of *A Mercy* is set on a farm and the owner is Jacob, who establishes an equal and harmonious relationship with the indentured laborers on his farm. His farm is described as a family for the homeless. As Morrison describes, on the farm, "each member dependent on them, none cruel, all kind" (*Mercy*, 144). To some degree, the farm is considered to be a paradise for them. However, this Eden-like farm begins to fall due to Jacob's avarice. The farm which is once a paradise is collapsed at last with Jacob's death. As Frye says in *The Great Code: the Bible and Literature*:

> There existing two roads in front of human beings. One was that human being went beyond the material world, the other was that human was captured by the material world, and thereby fell into the abyss of sin. (Frye, 1997: 151)

Unfortunately, Jacob chooses the death road of bloated material desires, which leads to his tragedy and death.

At the beginning of the story, on Jacob's farm, masters and slaves get along with each other harmoniously. They respect each other and work hard together to build their home. His farm becomes the refuge harbor, in which people coming from different races and classes live together with equality and freedom. However, such a peaceful land is not sustained when Jacob's benevolence is gradually devoured by his avarice. When he sees the splendid and grand house of the slave-owner, Jacob "in spite of himself, envied the house, the gate, the fence" and "fancying that one day, not too far away, to build a house that size on his own property" (27). In order to make more money, he travels a lot to expand his business, which leads to the deterioration of the farm. What is more, Jacob "hired men to help clear trees from a wide swath of land at the foot of a rise" (88) in order to build the house, as Lina mentioned, "Killing trees in that number, without asking their permission, of course, his efforts would stir up misfortune" (44). What Lina implies here is Jacob's cutting off the trees to meet his avarice destroys the nature. At last, Jacob consumes up all his energy to construct the house. But he falls sick when the construction is almost finished and dies before it is completed.

Jacob's avarice also leads to his estrangement from his wife. As his business becomes more successful, their communication becomes less. In the past, Jacob always brought small but practical presents for Rebekka as she wished when he came back from trade. However, when Jacob pays more attention to money and materials, he begins to bring back some useless and even weird presents. He does not care what his wife wants at all. Gradually, Rebekka loses interest in the gifts and thinks they are useless, even whimsical:

> A sliver tea service which was put away immediately; a porcelain chamber pot quickly chipped by discriminate use; a heavily worked hairbrush for hair he only saw in bed. A hat here; and a lace collar there. For yards of silk ... a mirror framed in silver. (88)

Now Jacob is more interested in his business, leaving Rebekka at home lonely with all these lavish gifts. It is the excessive avarice that destroys their happy marriage.

Jacob's farm is used to be a heaven of peace and happiness, staying away from disputes and evils of the world. Since he invests in plantation business, the farm has been infiltrated by materialism. He is no longer satisfied with his original house and makes every effort to construct the grand house. Unlimited material lust finally destroys him. Just like Einstein said:

> Wealth cannot help human beings make advances, which remains the same even if it is controlled by those who hold extreme warm-heartedness towards this course. Only the examples set by the great and pure personages can guide us to possess noble characters and behaviors. Money can only arouse one's selfishness, lead irresistibly to endless trouble, and even lead people off the right path. (Einstein, 1996: 37)

The heavy price Jacob pays for his avarice demonstrates Morrison's negative attitude towards the materialistic value. The reason behind Jacob's failure exactly corresponds with the concepts of Confucianism, the first one is his lack of "wisdom" (*zhi*, 智). Wisdom, originally written as (*zhi*, 知), a different Chinese characteristic representing knowing, means intelligence. It suggests a clear cognition and judgment of right and wrong, advantage, and disadvantage. Wisdom shows one's ability to distinguish right from wrong and make rational decisions facing temptation. Confucianism believes that people should have wisdom so as not to be confused by the complexities of life and be able to act with ethical and ritual standards. Jacob chooses to fulfill his material desire regardless of his ability and other people's needs, which shows his lack of wisdom.

Another Confucian notion "restraining desires" (*guayu*, 寡欲) is also reflected in this novel. The term means to reduce desires for external materials. Confucianism believes that human beings who pursue an excessive material desire is harmful to them, causing problems with others and lead to social disorders. In Confucianism, moral cultivation provides an important way to foster virtue and help people to restrain desires, and return to "a natural state". Just as Mencius said:

> The best way to conduct self-cultivation is to restrain desire. A person

with few desires may be lacking in virtue, but such loss is limited; a person
with many desires may still retain some virtue, but will lose much of it.
(*Mencius*, 1992: 210)

The above citation emphasizes when a human being's avarice and its roots
are eradicated in his mind, he returns to his natural existence in the world. He
would obtain the happiness of life in the process of returning to his own self. In
Jacob's case, his failure results from his unrestrained desire of constructing the
grand house without considering the authentic meaning of life. This section has
analyzed one of the reasons of the disharmonious relationship with the inner self.
That is the lack of morality and virtues. The next section moves on to discuss the
second reason behind the failure of self-identity construction: human's lack of self-
love and self-value.

4.1.2 Lack of Self-Love and Self-Value

Morrison describes the destructive forces of the white's values towards African
Americans, especially the African American women. Some are unable to realize
the beauty of their black images and fall into victims of the white's beauty standard.
In Morrison's works, she shows that internalized by the white culture, many
African Americans abandon their original cultural identity and even apply the
white cultural standards to judge their own culture. And the white's beauty standards
have been immersed into every aspect of African Americans' life, damaging their
construction of a harmonious relationship with the inner self. This part analyzes
the characters' lack of self-love and self-value in *The Bluest Eye, Tar Baby*, and *A
Mercy*.

Confucianism "unity of Heaven and human" regards self-love as an
important aspect of human self-realization. It holds that self-love is the basis for
one to love others. As Confucius says, "Respect yourself and others will respect
you." (Annping, 2014: 123) It means that a human being should value himself.

Once he is certain of his own value, he will surely be able to grow self-confidence within his inner self. If a human being does not accept his own value and existence in the world, it is impossible to construct self-identity as a human being. In order to construct a complete self-identity, human needs to start from loving and cherishing himself.

Unlike the white women who are oppressed mainly by white men, African American women are oppressed not only by white people but also by African American men. In a society dominated by the white culture and white beauty standard, African Americans are taught that blonde hair, blue eyes, and white skin is beautiful and superior. The oppressive white beauty standard promoted by media degrades their self-esteem. Many of Morrison's characters are internalized with the white beauty standard and rejecting their black image. Pecola and her mother, Pauline in *The Bluest Eye* are representative figures that lose self-identity because of the white beauty standard. In Jane Kuenz's essay, "*The Bluest Eye*: Notes on History, Community, and Black Females Subjectivity"(1994), she asserts that the displacement in the larger society deprives the black community of its supportive networks and produces a group of individuals who are, at times, painfully alienated from each other as each is divided within his inner self, which is the source of Pecola's split consciousness. The author totally agrees with Jane Kuenz's words. While the essay only deals with the role of community in their self-identity construction. In the following section, this book explores other reasons for their self-destruction. That is their lack of self-love and self-value.

The tragic story in *The Bluest Eye* demonstrates how terrible the white's beauty standard has affected African Americans, especially the little girls. Pecola grows up with the hatred of her parents and despise of other people. She attributes her miserable life to her black skin and dreams of having a pair of blue eyes. Pecola believes the change of her outlook would make her get over the hatred and despise. She believes that so long as she possesses blue eyes, her parents would not quarrel and would love her. And her classmates and teachers would not despise her anymore. As Morrison describes, every day "long hours she sat looking in the mirror, trying to discover the secret of the ugliness, the ugliness that made her ignored or despised at school, by teachers and classmates alike" (*Bluest*, 45). Pecola attributes her misfortune to her ugliness, imagining that with blue eyes her living condition would be changed.

In the black community where Pecola lives, the aesthetics of the white culture has been internalized in people's mind. Some black women fail to realize the beauty of black skin and try to mime white women, such as their dressing and way of life. However, they are further disdained and discriminated against by other people. Pecola's mother, Pauline Breedlove, is a representative who has been rejected both by the white society and the black community. After moving to northern Kentucky, Pauline goes to the movies frequently as she is deeply attracted by the white's beauty standards presented in the films. She fixes her hair up, apart from on the side, with one little curl on the forehead, imitating the white people's way of life. She regards her black identity as the reason for her miserable life. Pauline transfers her dissatisfaction with life to her daughter, Pecola, which causes a fatal damage to Pecola's psychological health.

What is more, her relationship with Cholly has been distorted by her obsession with the lifestyle of the white people. In the face of the choice about whether to be dutiful for her family or transfer her love to the white family, Pauline chooses the latter and denies her identity as a black woman and mother. "She became what was known as an ideal servant, for such a role satisfied all of her need practically." (100) For Pauline, she gets rid of the humiliation of being a black woman by working in a white family. Her negative attitude toward black skin also has a deadly influence on Pecola.

Like her mother, Pecola is also internalized with the aesthetic values of the dominant white society and denies her black identity. There are many white images in Pecola's lives. For instance, the white stars as Marry Jane, Shirley Temple, and Jane Withers, and so on. She takes "every opportunity to drink milk out of it just to handle and see sweet Shirley's face" (23). And for Pecola, "to eat the candy is somehow to eat the eyes, eat Mary Jane. Love Mary Jane. Be Mary Jane" (50). Also, there are white dolls with blue eyes, yellow hair, and pink skin. These white images exert a subtle influence on Pecola's mind and she is consumed by the white's standard of beauty. She gradually believes that the girls with blue eyes and yellow hair are beautiful and blackness is ugly and inferior. For her, a pair of blue eyes represent a kind of privilege:

> It had occurred to Pecola some time ago that if their eyes, those eyes that held the pictures, and knew the sights—if those eyes of her were different, that is to say, beautiful, she herself would be different. (46)

She believes that if she is beautiful with a pair of blue eyes, her parents would stop to fight with each other and she is able to live a happy life. However, the ending of the novel is a tragedy. Pecola ends up being schizophrenic and hallucinates that she has been granted the blue eyes. She goes further and further away from her true self and finally loses her self-identity.

The white ideology has distorted African Americans' psychology so deeply that they despise themselves, believing their miserable life derives from their black skin and black identity. The longing for blue eyes gradually deprives Pecola of her dignity, self-confidence, and her identity. The wish consumes her mind and destroys her spirit. Pauline and Pecola are destructed by the white's values due to their self-hatred and lack of self-love. Their tragic experience is caused by their lack of the Confucian concept of "sincerity" (*cheng*, 诚), which means being truthful without deceit. Confucianism believes that sincerity is the root and foundation of morality. All moral deeds must be conducted based on sincerity from the bottom of the heart. Otherwise, they are nothing but pretensions. *The Doctrine of the Mean* maintains, "Nothing can be achieved without sincerity." Sages are sincere by nature. *Junzi* (君子, a man of virtue) upholds sincerity as his goal for moral attainment and an approach to achieving the "way of Heaven" and the "principles of Heaven". Sincerity is the basis for other morality, just as the following statement in *A Collection of Doctrine of the Mean*:

> Only the most complete sincere person under Heaven, he can fully develop his human nature. Able to fully develop his nature, he can fully develop the nature of others. Able to develop the nature of others, he willfully achieves the nature of all things. Able to develop the nature of all things, he will assist the transformation and nourishing of Heaven and Earth. Able to assist the transformation and nourishing of Heaven and Earth, he may form a ternion with Heaven and Earth. (Wang & Wen, 2013: 334)

Due to their lack of sincerity, it is impossible for them to be true to themselves and realize their own beauty and love by themselves.

In *Tar Baby*, Morrison once again mentions the internalized beauty standard of the African Americans which occurred in *The Bluest Eye*. Morrison also explores African American women's pursuit of self-awareness in this novel. Moreover, she describes the long-existing contradiction of the black and white cultures in American society. The conflict of Son and Jadine is primarily attributed to their different value systems. Jadine is a black girl who has absorbed the white culture and values. When she was two years old, Jadine lost her father, and her mother died ten years later. She was adopted by her uncle Sydney and his wife Ondine, living with their white owner, Valerine. During her growing stage, Jadine accepted the education of the white culture and regarded the white value is superior over the blacks. Her mind is full of white cultural values and refuses to accept the black culture. However, as African Americans are only considered as "the other" in the white-dominated society, it is difficult for her to establish self-identity without cultural roots in society. Influenced by the white's standard of beauty and values, Jadine always adopts the white's beauty standard to judge people. For instance, when Jadine is attracted by an African American woman with asphalt skin wearing a canary yellow dress in Paris, she comments, "Under her long canary yellow dress Jadine knew there was much hip, too much bust." (45) Jadine takes the white's beauty standard as the only criteria to evaluate people.

Morrison adopts the image of a tar baby to signify Jadine, who worsens her situation with more efforts to immerse herself into the white culture. She compares Jadine to a "cultural orphan":

> She (Jadine) is cut off. She does not have her ancient properties; she does not have what Ondine has. There is no reason for her to be like Ondine—I'm not recommending that—but she needs a little bit of Ondine to be a complete woman. There should be a quality of adventure and nest. (Taylor-Guthrie, 1994: 104)

Jadine has discarded her black cultural identity under the influence of the white civilization. The notion that the white is noble and elegant but the black is inferior and vulgar has always been instilled in her mind. She wants to abandon the black culture that causes her loss of a sense of belonging in the black community. When Jadine goes to Eloe, Son's hometown, she almost does not know how to communicate with other people. In Jadine's eyes, Eloe is a place that is ignorant and backward. Jadine thinks that New York is the only place that she belongs to. Jadine becomes a cultural orphan who has no sense of belonging in either the black culture or the white culture, which accounts for her spiritual barrenness and loss of self-identity.

Another character in this novel is Alma, who has also been influenced by the white culture. She believes that the shiny hair of the white is beautiful and fashionable while the curly hair of the black is ugly. Alma always wants to have a red wig. She thinks that she would be as pretty as the white girl wearing a red wig. In fact, a red wig does not fit her well, just like "a bougainvillea in a girdle, like a baby jaguar with lipsticks on, like an avocado with earrings" (242). she looks weird with these fashionable things. Like Jadine, Alma tries to exclude the black culture and immerse herself in the white-dominated society. However, it is difficult for her to be truly accepted by the white society. She suffers from a sense of spiritual loneliness in her deep heart. Both Jadine and Alma are cultural orphans without a self-identity as they try to cast away their own culture. Their loss of self-identity is caused by denying their black identity and loss of self-value. Self-value refers to an individual's affirmation of self-existence and the definition of self-worth. It reflects the acceptance of oneself to give enough attention to one's inner self, and it asks one to live according to his own judgment rather than others' and takes responsibility for his own life. Jadine and Alma live with the white people's values and fail to recognize their own beauty and value as African American women. Their life is affected easily by other people's judgment and behaviors, which inevitably leads to their loss of self-identity.

Florens in *A Mercy* is another typical representative who losses her self-identity because of her lack of self-love and self-value. Her mother leaft her when she was very young. "Mother discarded her for keeping her little brother who still sucks the breast, and that casts a shadow over her mind forever; when Florens in pain, and in horror, she would think of that." Obviously, abandoned by her mother, Florens has experienced a great pain in her mind and loses confidence in live. As we all know, maternal love plays an important role in the formation of children's personalities. The desertion by her mother makes Florens feel inferior to others. After arriving at Jacob's farm, Florens tries to please others for fear of being abandoned or discarded by other people. Lina describes her as, "Florens had been a quiet, timid version of herself at the time of her displacement." (*Mercy,* 61) People around her feel that she is the "combination of defenselessness, eagerness to please, and most of all, a willingness to blame herself for the meanness of others" (152). Because of the lack of love and affection, "She was deeply grateful for every shred of affection, any pat on the head, any smile of approval" (61). It is the fear of being abandoned that makes her act like that. Florens has completely lost her self-value and submitted to anyone in her life without any criterion, which foreshadows the iron smith's abandonment.

In the love relationship with the black iron smith, Florens puts herself in an inferior position. She fell in love with him when she was 16 years old and viewed him "as my life and my security from harm, from any who look closely at me only to throw me away. From all those who believe they have a claim and rule over me" (157). She puts herself in a subordinate position and is willing to be a slave in love. The psychological trauma caused by her mother's abandonment in childhood makes Florens yearn for love. In her confession, Florens recalls that she has seen a stag rambling in the forest. For the first time, she senses the taste of freedom; however, she is reluctant to be free from her lover:

> I wonder what else the world may show me. It is as though I am loose
> to do what I choose, the stag, the wall of flowers. I am a little scared of this
> looseness. Is that how free feels; I don't like it. I don't want to be free of
> you. (70)

She has completely lost independence and self-value in front of love, which is destined to be abandoned by her lover. Although Lina warns her against the fact that "you are one leaf on his tree", Florens answers, "No, I am his tree." (61)

Afterward, when she is sent to seek the iron smith to treat her owner Rebekka's illness, Florens finds that her lover has adopted an orphan named Malaik. Then he leaves Florens staying at home to take care of the little boy. Florens is so jealous of the close relationship between the iron smith and the little boy, so when Malaik damages her shoes, she fights with him. After the iron smith returns, he beats Florens and kicks her out of the door. When Florens asks the reason, he tells her, "Your head is empty and your body is wild." (141) The reason why the iron smith refuses to accept Florens' love is not that she is a slave, but that Florens has "no mind" at all. What the iron smith says shows a truth that Florens has lost her self-value and her mind is in a state of being enslaved unconsciously. Without awareness of self-love and self-value, she is prone to lose her judgment and become a victim of self-degradation.

So far this section has focused on human's disharmonious relation with self in Morrison's three novels. Through analyzing the character's experience and fate, this book makes a conclusion that there are mainly two reasons for human's loss of self-identity: their lack of morality and virtues, and lack of self-love and self-value. In contrast to the loss of self-identity caused by the characters' disharmonious relationship with their inner self, the author moves on to examine the characters' construction of a harmonious relationship with the inner self, which is the basis for their construction of self-identity.

4.2 Construction of Harmonious Relationship with Self

Morrison depicts many representative characters with an independent self-identity and shapes them as spiritual leaders to other black people. Those people successfully construct a harmonious relationship with the inner self because of their possession of morality and virtues as well as self-love and self-value. Confucian "unity of Heaven and human" advocates that to be an exemplary person require morality and virtues. It is the fundamental requirement of being a human. At the same time, one should have the awareness of self-love and self-value and reflect the value of existence in the world. In this part, the author examines Morrison's characters' exploration of morality and virtues and self-love and self-value in the process of constructing their self-identity, and finally achieving harmony with their inner self.

4.2.1 Exploration of Morality and Virtues

Confucian "unity of Heaven and human" puts forward that morality and virtues are crucial in interaction with others, which helps them to achieve self-realization. Confucius believes that "self-reform can come about only through the influence of moral instruction and exemplary virtue" (Annping, 2014: 16). This is true in the characters depicted by Morrison who has completed their self-identity construction by the possession of morality and virtues. They worship and love their own culture and pursue self-value boldly. Morrison depicts these women as "industrious" "considerate", and "filled with wisdom". Although they live in poverty, they never give up their ideal and dreams. They try to seek their own value and evaluate themselves with the black cultural standard rather than with the white ones; they are strong and tolerant, and dedicate their love to others. Confucius believes that "the moral resolve of a few could favorably affect the fate of many" (Annping, 2014: 37). Just like nature, they provide spirit nutriment and guidance for other people. Suffering from oppression and exploitation of the patriarchal culture, they still have a firm belief and work together to make a better and hopeful life. In this section, the author adopts the representative characters, such as L in *Love*, Consolata in *Paradise*, and Bride in *God Help the Child* to demonstrate their exploration of morality and virtues in constructing their self-identities.

In *Love*, there are only a few characters that appear in the Cosey family: L. Vida, Sandler—former workers in the Cosey family, Roman and Junior—people who now work for the family. The novel starts 25 years after Cosey's death in 1990 when he still has an influence on the relationship between everybody with others in the family. In this novel, Morrison creates an outstanding African American woman image, whose name is L. Some critics hold the view that L is the abbreviation of "love". L is tolerant and full of love towards other people. She has worked in the Cosey family for nearly 50 years and witnessed the love and hatred between the Cosey women. She is an observer of this family, protecting the Cosey women in her way, "L was the only peacemaker around, whether glaring or shaking her head, but she would take no one's side" (*Love*, 133). Out of love, she does not want to see the misunderstanding and fight between these women and tries her best to coordinate the relationships between them. In L's view, they have their shortcomings like selfishness and jealousy. All their fights start because "each had been displaced by another; each has a unique claim on Cosey's affection" (98). It seems that the deficiency of love between them is attributed to the only man—Cosey, "He was the big man who, with no one to stop him, could get away with it and anything else he wanted" (133). In addition, Heed and Christine turn into enemies also because of Bill Cosey's marriage with Heed, and the two girls are:

> Once—perhaps twice-a-year, they punched grabbed hair, wrestled, bit, slapped. Never drawing blood, never apologizing, never premeditating, yet drawn annually to pant through an episode that was as much rite as the fight. (73)

When Cosey is alive, they fight for the favor of him; after Cosey's death, they contend for the property that Cosey left to prove his love for them. L understands them because of her awareness of their plight in the patriarchal Cosey family.

L believes that these women should love each other and unite together to fight for their own identity. She tries her best to protect them, and the whole Cosey family secretly. When Heed is taken by Cosey as his second wife, Christine and her mother May "went wild just thinking about his choice of a UP Beach girl for his bride" (75). And when Heed moves into the Cosey family, she is alienated by them. What's worse, on her wedding day, May and Christine keep laughing at and criticizing her behaviors. "May and her daughter moved on to relentless criticism of the young bride: her speech, hygiene, table manners, and thousands of things Heed didn't know." (76) It is L "who liked her in those days, taught her a lot, and saved the life Papa had given her and her alone. She could never have navigated those treacherous waters if L hadn't been the current" (76).

Another evident example is when Mr. Cosey hits Heed because of her quarrel with Christine at Christine's birthday party, L taps him on the shoulder and said, "Don't you ever lay a hand on her again no matter what. Do and I'm long gone." (141) Mr. Cosey admits his misbehavior to Heed and says he will never hit Heed again. Moreover, L always teaches Heed how to behave in a right way, when Heed asks Christine to wear her wedding ring, L turned on her "watch yourself" and "the streets don't go there" (129), teaching her it is wrong and impolite to do this. L is sympathetic to this poor girl and gives her the warmth in this cold family.

Except for Heed, Christine also has a closer relationship with L than with her mother. Christine's father died when she was five years old. During the funeral, people kept coming to comfort the parents and the widow, but nobody cared about Christine's sorrow. As L's recalls, with fear and loneliness:

> Christine crawled under my bed, and when I found her there, I let her sleep with me, she was never a crying child, so listening to her whimpering in her sleep was a comfort to me since May looked on Billy Boy's death as more of an insult than a tragedy. Dry-eyed as a turtle, she left Christine to me to raise. (137)

Christine gains a sense of protection and security with L. In contrast, her mother, May does not take her responsibility for Christine. She devotes her whole life to the Cosey family to delight the Cosey men, "Her whole life was making sure those Cosey men had what they wanted. The father more than the son; the father more than her daughter" (102). She is also strict with Christine:

> [Christine] had hated her mother for expelling her from her bedroom and, when Chief Buddy brought her back, smacking her face so hard Christine's can hit her shoulder. The slap sent her into hiding under L's bed for two

days. (96)

To Christine, "May wasn't much a mother to me" (184) and L is the only person who cared and loved her at the time. L saved Christine's life when Heed tries to burn Christine's bed after their fierce fight. It was L who smothered the blackened sheets with a twenty-pound sack of sugar. What is more, L protected May from Heed:

> According to May's letters, as far back as 1960 Heed had begun to research ways to put her in a restroom or an asylum. But nothing Heed did could force May out. With L watching and without an accomplice, Heed failed. (99)

L also took care of Cosey's funeral while other Cosey women focused on fighting for the property. "Had it not been for L, the county's role model would never have gotten the dignified funeral he deserved." (37) At Bill Cosey's funeral, these Cosey women fought over his coffin, Heed tried to stab Christine with a knife and was stopped by L, "Once again L restored order, just as she always had" (34). L always appears in a dangerous and emergent situation, protecting the Cosey women with her braveness and wisdom. Knowing that Mr. Cosey left all the Cosey property to his mistress, Celestial, L thought:

> It wasn't right ... I wasn't going to let him put his family put in the street. May was sixty-one, what was she supposed to do? Spend her old age in a straitjacket? And Heed was almost forty-one. Was she supposed to go back to a family who had not spoken to her since Truman? And Christine— whatever she was into wasn't going to last. (201)

She forges Bill Cosey's will to leave his property to these poor women who have contributed all their life to this family. She is not only a peacemaker but a protector of these black women.

L keeps a close relationship with other people with her love and affection for everyone. She bears the morality of benevolence, responsibility, courage, and wisdom, acting as a spiritual leader to guide other black women out of the predicament in a patriarchal society. All the Cosey women are victims of the oppression from the patriarchal power. It is with L's love that the hatred and misunderstanding between the Cosey women dissolve at last. L acts like the exemplary person in Confucian "unity of Heaven and human" with morality and virtues, achieving self-realization as well as guiding the well-being of other people's life.

Consolata in *Paradise,* like L, is the mentor of the whole Convent community. She unites the black women together with morality and virtues. Consolata was rescued by Mother at the age of nine and then became a pious nun under Mother's guide. After the betrayal of her lover Deacon and the death of Mother, Consolata feels depressed and self-contempt. But she chooses to become "Consolata Sosa", a healer who provides her love to other Convent women. At first, these women regard each other as intruders of their territory, and the relationship between them is unfriendly and tense.

Mavis is the first to come to the Convent, and she regards herself as the elder sister in Convent. When Gigi comes here, Mavis thinks, "No way, no way at all. Mother's gone, but Connie's okay. I've been here for almost three years, and this house is where we are. Us. Not her." (*Paradise*, 77) Gigi always wears the scantiest outfits, flirts with young men, and sunbathes herself nakedly in the yard of Convent. Mavis despises Gigi and regards her as a "whore". When these girls come back from K. D's wedding, Mavis and Gigi are fighting so fiercely that they nearly get naked in Mavi's Cadillac:

> The Cadillac rocked. Gigi was scrappy but vain—she didn't want bruises or scratches to mar her lovely face and she worried constantly about her hair.

Mavis was slow but steady, joyful hitter. When Gigi saw blood, she assumed it was her own and scrambled from the car, Mavis scooting after her. Under a metal-hot void of even one arrow if birds they fought on the road and its shoulder. (168)

At that time, Mavis and Gigi fail to show sympathy and compassion to each other. They do not respect each other and refuse to share their feelings and stories. These girls hate and resent each other. Then, Consolata tells other girls her personal story. She has been tortured by the physical desire and spiritual belief. As a nun, she should be pure in spirit; however, she has been seduced to be a mistress in the past, which split her into two parts by depression. Until she becomes a "magic healer" under Mother's instruction, she finally puts her split selves together.

Consolata transforms herself from a woman who blames herself all day to a "new and revised Reverend Mother" in Convent and becomes the spiritual mentor of other women. She guides them to reveal their innermost feelings, emotions, and unspeakable experiences, which helps them walk out of the shadow of their devastating past and establish a mutual understanding relationships between them. Eventually, these women step out of their past and share their sufferings with other women, and recognize their beloved part of the authentic self.

They all have been maltreated and deserted by society, so at the very beginning, they close their heart for fear of being hurt again. After sharing their unfortunate experiences, they begin to trust and understand other people and turn to be considerate and helpful under Consolata's influence. The stories of the Convent women have been unraveled, the loud dreaming has been shared by all, and various confessions have been made. A communion is established successfully, which facilitates these women to purge and eventually purify their own self. Because of the mutual understanding, those women accept and appreciate the differences that used to cause conflicts between them. Finally, they liberate themselves from the past, enjoy the peace and freedom from their inner heart and build a sisterhood with each other.

The Convent women successfully convert pain into mutual nurturing. With the help of Consolata, they make Convent an ideal place for the heart-broken women. The Covent women have remarkable patience to comfort others and provide security to those poor women. Consolata is regarded as an "ideal parent, friend, and companion". She helps other women to relieve their distress and pressure:

> This sweet, unthreatening old lady who seemed to love each one of the best, who never criticized, who shared everything but needed little or no care; required no emotional investment; who listened to; who locked no doors and accepted each as she was. (262)

As a spiritual healer to other women in Convent, Consolata arouses the awareness of morality and virtues of the Convent women. They build a free community with non-hierarchical, non-racial, and non-patriarchal. They have made it an equal place that is free from all kinds of discrimination and prejudice which contributes to these women's sound development of personality.

As was mentioned in the previous two novels, Morrison depicts two spiritual leaders with morality and virtues. The final part of this section examines the protagonist in *God Help the Child*, Bride, who completes her exploration of morality by realizing mistakes and finally compensating for her mistakes. And she finally possesses the morality of "wisdom" and "sincerity" in Confucianism. Bride, an African American woman, lives in a family without parental love. In order to get attention and affirmation from her mother, Bride acts obediently by to Sweetness, "I behaved and behaved and behaved." (*God Help the Child*, 32) She tries her best to make Sweetness happy and does whatever her mother asks. Even when she happens to see the landlord Mr. Leigh's abusing a little white boy,

Sweetness asks her, "Don't you say a word about it, not to anybody." (54) For fear of being driven out by the landlord, Bride listens to her mother's word but puts an innocent teacher, Sofia Huxley, into prison for fifteen years. This mistake has haunted Bride for the rest of her life with remorse.

The guilty of framing innocent Sofia Huxley never stops haunting her. She can't focus on anything, losing interest in everything; she can't read, feeling dizzy about the printing; she does not bear to listen to music, as she said, "I am not sure which is worse, being dumped like trash or whipped like a slave." (29) Bride is haunted by grieve and guilty of her mistake. To get out of the trauma, Bride starts to have awareness of being true to herself initially as she can be. She knows clearly that she must make up for her mistakes to regain her inner peace. "All my life, I was trying to make up to someone I ruined." (154) Adult Bride decides to compensate for her mistake to reduce her guilt, so she said, "I guess I want to feel good about myself. Not so disposable." (49)

Bride makes a plan to help Sofia with five thousand dollars in cash and three-thousand-dollar tickets, hoping these can help Sofia with her tough life. When she meets Sofia at the prison, Bride offers a lift to Sofia. However, just released from prison with fear, Sofia refuses her help without recognizing Bride. After following Sofia to her house, Bride tries her best to offer her presents. With inner struggling, Bride tells Sofia that she is the blue-black girl Lula Ann who framed her as a molester on the court and now she is here for help. Suffering from fifteen years of humiliating life in the prison, Sofia is extremely angry with Bride's appearance. She could not help herself beating, kicking, and punching Bride. Sofie regards Bride as a devil, "I was ripping blue-and-white wallpaper, returning slaps and running the devil Mommy knew so well out of my life." (77) Beaten by Sofia, Bride chooses not to fight back. "I did not make a sound, did not even raise a hand to protect myself." (70) She just lies there, whimpering, trembling, and doing nothing. Bride does not call the police, just calls her friend Brooklyn for help instead. After beating Bride, Sofie realizes that "Freedom is never free.

You have to fight for it. Make for it and make sure you can handle it". She gets relieved and realizes that freedom is earned by nobody but herself. "That black girl did do me a favor." (70) Eventually, Sofia has forgiven Bride.

Bride properly sublimates the sense of morality and realizes moral redemption. She is aware of the sense of guilt, responsibility, mercy, and love. She realizes her mistake and chooses to be true to herself, accepting her mistake and makes up for it. Her behavior corresponds with the Confucian concept of "wisdom" and "sincerity", as she admits her mistake by differentiating right from wrong, and chooses to be true to herself. Confucius once said:

> If a man of position [junzi] does not have integrity, he will not inspire
> awe. And when he tries to learn, he will not persevere to the end. Such a
> man should stay close to those who do their best and are trustworthy. He
> should not befriend those who are not his equals. And when he makes a
> mistake, he should not be afraid to correct it. (Annping, 2014: 38)

Confucius holds that the most important for an exemplary person is to know to correct his mistakes, which is also most difficult to carry out. It is "not the same as expressing regret about his mistake or even blaming himself for it", and it is when he is alone, he is able to "see himself honestly" and "grasp the urgency of self-reform" (Annping, 2014: 115). Finally, Bride learns the morality of being true to self and honesty. She manages to explore the moral truth, attempts to establish normal morality, and realizes moral salvation. During the period of self-reform, Bride finally distinguishes from right and wrong, from truth and false. When Bride understands her mistakes and starts to make up for it, she has the sense of morality and virtues.

4.2.2 Awareness of Self-Love and Self-Value

Having defined morality and virtues as the first aspect of establishing self-identity to achieve harmony with the inner self, the second aspect refers to the possession of self-love and self-value. In the last section, characters' possession of self-love and self-value in *Paradise* and *God Help the Child* is examined.

For more than three hundred years, African Americans have been told that they are ugly and inferior, and their dignity and value have been degraded and denied by the white-dominated society. What's worse, their children have been treated with the prejudice that they are ugly, inferior, and insignificant. Most of them lack the sense of self-love and self-value, which cause their loss of self-identity. For African Americans, loving their bodies is the first step to love their own self. The body has a special meaning for them who suffered from slavery. It is the greatest desire for them to have free control of their bodies, especially for the African American women who live with the sexual oppression of the whites. Confucian "unity of Heaven and human" also advocates that loving and protecting one's body is the basis to establish one's self hood. It holds that one should bear the responsibility to cherish his body for being a benevolent person to love himself. Self-love contains the meaning of loving their own race culture, which is a basis for their survival. The black race culture is fundamental for them to establish their self-identity in the hybrid culture society.

In *Paradise*, thanks to Consolata's guide and the Convent women's self-awareness, they have successfully realized the unification of their body and spirit. All of them have been confronted with different predicaments before seeking refuge in Convent. For example, Mavis is the first one to come to Convent with terrible physical and psychological traumas. Her husband treats her as personal property and beats her with violence, and she also receives contempt from the community. All of these sufferings lead to her loss of self-love and self-value as a human being. Mavis escapes from her home to Convent with a belief that "she was the dumbest bitch on the planet" (*Paradise*, 37). She has lost her sense of self-worth and dignity due to her husband and other people's abuse and oppression. Another woman, Gigi, is the victim of racial discrimination and constantly haunted by the death of the black boy killed by the police in the racial conflict. "Sirens, yes, and distant bullhorns, but of breaking glass, nobody slams, no gunfire. So why did a map of red grow on the little boy's white shirt?" (170) Since then, Gigi finds her life is meaningless and searches for existence by having sex with a man.

As to Seneca, she is harassed by the lack of family love. She was abandoned by her mother when she was a child, and she was sent to different foster families. In the foster families, Seneca was harassed by her foster brother and formed a strange habit of scratching and cutting her skin to win affection from her foster mother. The lack of love and affection from her mother has split her body and soul. Another girl, Pallas is frustrated with the adultery between her boyfriend and her mother. What is worse, she is raped by a stranger, aggravating her situation. Women in Convent all have been maltreated by other people and have suffered from psychological trauma. Their self-esteem, self-value, and pride have been trampled upon with a split spiritual world. They all fail to recognize the beauty of their bodies and lose hope for the future. However, under Consolata's instruction, they all successfully rebuild their self-identity through a "magic" drawing by realizing the beauty and the importance of their body. The drawing works like:

> First with natural features: breasts and pudenda, toes, ears, and head hair. Seneca duplicated in robin's egg blue one of her more elegant scars, one drop of red at its tip. Later on, when she had the hunger to slice her inner thigh, she chose instead to mark the open body lying on the cellar floor. (265)

During the process of drawing a woman's body on the cellar floor, they understand the meaning of "my body is nothing my spirit everything" (270). After knowing the importance of the body, they stop restricting themselves in the shackles of flesh and start to realize the beauty of their bodies. They begin to gain the awareness of loving themselves with an independent soul. By cherishing their bodies first, then they realize the importance of spirit in their identity construction. They become tender and considerate and begin to communicate with each other, and finally, achieve mutual understanding with other people.

The Convent women possess a sense of self-love and self-value under Consolata's guidance. Eventually, they start to recover from the panic experience, reconstruct their unique identity as a human being, and to accept their whole selves with body and soul united. After several years, Mavis had changed from a timid and dumb woman to a confident and independent woman who restores her freedom and identity mentally and physically. And Seneca finally realizes that she is independent and does not need her mother's love and affection any more; Gigi knows what to do to become an adorable person rather than use some inappropriate tricks. Finally, she turns to be an elegant and righteous woman in Convent. In this novel, Consolata is the soul character to guide the Convent women out of their spiritual predicament and realize their reconstruction of self-identity. The pilgrimage of the self-identity construction starts from their realization of the body beauty, their efforts to overcome patriarchal power, and their search for self-identity. The description of these Convent women naturally lead the readers to the conclusion that self-love and self-value are the basis for one's free identity construction.

Different from her previous novels, in *God Help the Child*, Morrison portraits the character who manages to take "Black is the new Black" (33), and accepts the black skin as a blessing rather than a curse. Lula Ann Bridewell is one of the outstanding African American female characters. After leaving Sweetness, she starts to have an initial awareness of subjectivity—her identity as an African American female. She turns from Lula Ann Bridewell to Bride. At the beginning of the novel, Bride is self-loathing about her dark skin. In her view, "Lula" and "-well" sound stupid, revealing her identity as an African American black girl. She changes her name to Ann Bride as soon as she left school. Because of her shame as an African American woman, when she looks for a job, she is even unwilling to appear in front of the public. And after many refusals, she finally gets a job as a stock keeper.

Accidentally, Bride follows the designer Jeri's advice of wearing white clothes only. She finds that her total blackness outstanding in contrast with the white dressing. She suddenly realizes that her dark black skin is a blessing. When the two colors are put together, the contrast between black skin and white clothes makes Bride look shining in front of people. Due to the decoration of white clothes, the black skin shows its own charming. The combination of Bride's black skin and the white dress accentuates the unique beauty of Bride, she "makes people think of whipped cream and chocolate soufflé every time they see you" (33). Later, she is praised as more beautiful than the white girls for the first time. "White girls, even brown girls have to strip naked to get that kind of attention." (36)

Bride is confident of her blackness now. She believes that her dark black is an outstanding beauty, "not a strut, not that pelvis—out rush of the runway—but a stride, slow and focuses" (36). Her dark skin also helps her in career and she is promoted as a regional manager in Sylvia Inc. at last, Bride shortens her name from Ann Bride to Bride directly and now she has her own cosmetic line which is one of the top six in the cosmetic industry. In addition, Bride names her brand after "YOU, GIRL" that sells cosmetics for girls and women regardless of color "from ebony to lemonade to milk" (10). Bride has gained the confidence of her self-identity as an African American, and she is never self-loathing of her dark blackness anymore. She becomes a successful African American woman in business and has changed from the self-degraded Lula Ann Bridewell to confident Bride. It is a great progress for Bride to gain her sense of self-love and self-value, which drives her to be more confident and positive about life. Bride has proved that black skin is as beautiful as white.

As described on the previous pages, this chapter deals with the relationship between human and the inner self, which is the basis of human's construction of self-identity. In order to become a complete human being, one needs to possess morality and virtues as well as the sense of self-love and self-value. Without these human would suffer from spiritual barrenness and loss of self-identity. Confucian "unity of Heaven and human" also emphasizes that an exemplary person has morality and virtues as well as the ability to love his own. In this chapter, the author has attempted to provide various examples to prove that the Confucian ideas have been demonstrated in Morrison's works. The next chapter moves on to the conclusion of this book, in which the author summarizes the main research findings of this book as well as the significance of this study.

5

Conclusion

The examination throughout this study clarifies that Confucian thought "unity of Heaven and human" influences Toni Morrison's writing in various ways. The research of her novels leads to the conclusion that the three categories of relationships of Confucian "unity of Heaven and human" have been fully demonstrated by Morrison in her novels.

As a late-twentieth-century African American female writer, Morrison undertakes the cultural and artistic representation of the life and history of the African Americans. She speaks out against the triple burden of race, class, and gender of human beings. She shows deep concerns in motherhood, identity, gender and sexual relationships, family, culture, etc., which are closely connected with the survival and existence of human. Her work:

> Validate the black culture and reaffirms adaptive survival power, its creativity amidst oppression, life-affirming qualities; as well as its ancient wisdom and humanity and its capacity for survival. (Reed, 1988: 63)

As an astute scholar and a creative writer, Morrison has become an increasingly important voice of African Americans and of the "common voice" of human beings. She has won the deepest respect and admiration of both the writers and readers. Although her works are addressed mainly to the black readership, they have been read throughout the English-speaking world and beyond. Her works encourage critical thinking about our existence in a wealthy and fast-developing society, and give us the philosophical wisdom for life.

Some of her novels show us unusual scenes and crazy persons. Such as dogs speaking human language, an African American girl wishes for a pair of blue eyes, a father rapes his daughter, etc. Such scenes are connected with the normal and natural life. The connections are set up between these unusual events/characters and her identity as an African American humanistic writer. Her novels show her concerns about human beings' existence and development in the world. She explores human existence in the natural world, human interrelationships in society as well as human inner world, which are related to human self-identity construction. And it paves the way for the author's research on Confucian "unity of Heaven and human" in her literary career. Though as an oriental woman, her works transcend cultures and deeply touch the author's heart and inspire the author's imagination. Through bicultural reading of her works, the author has found rich connotations of Confucianism regarding the relationships between nature, human, society, and the inner self. As a result, this book came into being.

Confucian "unity of Heaven and human" provides a guidance of relationship-construction, unification, and harmonizing. With the rapid development of modern science and technology, the authentic harmonious relations between human and nature, between people, and between human with the inner self have been destroyed or distorted. People with different skin colors, cultural beliefs, and value judgments are disdained and discriminated against by others. Confucianism mainly focuses on morality, family loyalty, kindness and how to live an impact and meaningful life. It plays an important role in guiding human to gain a balance between material and spiritual progress. It also provides precious teachings in dealing with the disharmonious relationships between nature, human, and self which promote human growth and social development.

This book summarizes the definition and main ideas of Confucian "unity of Heaven and human". It includes three dimensions of relationships between human and nature, human and society, human and self. Concerning the relationship between human and nature, it asks reciprocal respect with each to realize mutual development. Human should respect and protect nature as well as make proper use of nature for their benefits within appropriate limits. At the same time, nature provides material and spiritual support for human survival. It is the basic and foremost relationship in the universe. Regarding the relationship between human and society, this book takes the familial relation and social relation as the basic discussion. In familial relations, the parents-children relationship is the most important one for children's physical and psychological development. It asks for mutual love and respect for each other to maintain a harmonious familial environment. What is more, human's interaction and relation with others in society are also of great importance. "Unity of Heaven and human" advocates that everyone needs to interact with social relations to become a complete human being. With regards to the relationship between human and the inner self, "unity of Heaven and human" proposes that human needs morality and virtues to restrain their desires. And self-love and self-value contribute to their construction of self-identity. "Unity of Heaven and human" revolves around nature, human, society, and the inner self, pursuing the highest goal of a harmonious relationship among them.

Morrison blends reality with myth, and contemplates history and real problems in a real and imagined world. Her works bear the characteristics of poetic language, superb narrative skill, and a strong sense of history. What's more, Morrison focuses on the process of individual growth as well as explores the destiny of the black race and the whole of humankind. Her writing on issue of race reflects the living conditions of African Americans, which ultimately leads to the universal state of humankind. Because of her African American identity, she pays more attention to African Americans and takes them as her characters in her works. She demonstrates that human's disharmonious and distorted relationship with nature, society, and self are the main reason for their natural, social, and spiritual crisis. At the same time, she depicts some representative characters that have successfully overcome similar survival crisis by maintaining a harmonious and close relationship with nature, society, and self, and finally constructing their self-identity.

The author analyzes Toni Morrison's works from the above-mentioned three aspects of relationships between nature, human, and self. This book explores the correspondence between "unity of Heaven and human" and the idea of Toni Morrison. Morrison advocates the return to nature where people could obtain spiritual support and wholesome state of mind. At the same time, Confucian "unity of Heaven and human" proposes the coexistence of human and nature. The relationship between human and society contains the parents-children relation, relation between different racial groups, and relation between the same race. Morrison points out that people should treat other people with love and respect. Everyone needs to establish a harmonious relationship with family members and other people in the society to construct his self-identity. Concerning the relationship between body and mind, to achieve harmony with the inner self is the ultimate and highest goal of "unity of Heaven and human" and Toni Morrison. The above analysis brings the following conclusions.

Human beings' close connection with nature has been undermined during the process of industrialization and commercialization, which causes a catastrophic impact on their living conditions as well as psychological development. Nature not only provides human with material resources but also is the spiritual home for human beings. In Morrison's works, nature occupies an important position in her story construction. An vivid description of the natural world appears in her novels to show human's relationship with the natural world. Morrison pays attention to describe the disharmonious and harmonious relationship between nature and human in her works. The disharmonious relationship is mainly demonstrated by human's destruction and domination of nature along with alienation from nature. The typical example is the immigration of African Americans from the natural south to the industrialized northern cities. Their close connection with nature has been destroyed by the materialization and people are keen to pursue material accumulation even by exploiting natural resources ruthlessly.

Morrison describes and shows human's violent destruction and exploitation of nature, which leads to self-destruction. While at the same time, nature takes its revenge on human's destructive activities. Human's alienation from nature also leads to their psychological trauma in their lives. Human's disharmonious relationship with nature is vividly described by Morrison in *Song of Solomon, Tar Baby*, *Paradise*, *Love,* and *A Mercy*. The original state of a harmonious relationship with nature has been overshadowed by human desire and greed, which causes the physical and psychological crisis for human's development. Morrison also depicts some characters that keep a harmonious relationship with nature and able to get spiritual nourishment from nature. It is of great help to their construction of a sound self-identity. They keep the most natural way of living with few material needs, and they gain contentment and consolation from nature rather than from materials. The fate and life experience of these two opposite kinds of characters are different regarding their relationship with nature. Morrison pursues the harmonious development of human and nature and hopes to establish a world in which human and nature exist harmoniously, which is also the call of Confucian "unity of Heaven and human".

The social crisis described in Morrison's works refers to the deformed and alienated relationship between people in family and society. Industrialization drives human beings to pursue material needs and wealth, which ruins humanity and causes ruthless relations among people. Morrison keeps exploring the interrelated relationship between people in her novels and the ways for people to build a harmonious relationship in life. It is consistent with the exploration of the "unity of Heaven and human". Interpersonal relationships with other people are the confirmation of one's existence in society, and an individual needs to keep harmonious relationships with family members and others to construct his/her self-identity. Among social relations, familial relation with family members, especially with parents, is the foremost one that influences the physical and mental development of an individual's growth. On the one side, parents are supposed to provide love and respect as well as education for their children to grow into an upright person. On the other side, children should conduct filial piety to their parents, respect, and love their parents, which is the basic requirement for an individual to become a complete human being. In Morrison's novels, the description of father-child, mother-child relationships take up a large amount of space. Distorted paternal love and abnormal maternal love in *The Bluest Eye, Song of Solomon, Beloved, and God Help the Child* are demonstrated by Morrison to show the destructive impact of disharmonious familial relations on children's development. What's more, children's failure of filial piety to their parents also leads to their moral deterioration which impedes their self-growth.

In Morrison's *Sula, Song of Solomon, Paradise*, she describes different kinds of discriminated and distorted relationships in society, such as the relationship between the whites and the blacks, relationship among the black people, and the alienated relationship of an individual with the community. An individual can't live isolated by in society without interaction with other people. In *Home and Beloved and Song of Solomon*, characters' reconnection with other people in the community helps them to reconstruct their self-identity and retreat their meaning in life. It is of great significance for an individual to maintain a harmonious relationship with others in society. Morrison believes that the only way out for the people to resist discrimination and inequality lies in their unity and harmonious relationship with each other. Because during the process of interaction with other people in society, one learns how to get along with each other, how to love and respect each other, how to support each other no matter in good or bad situations. Toni Morrison, with her literary and cultural insight, advocates maintaining a harmonious, equal racial and cultural order. She hopes to make a peaceful interracial and intraracial environment to seek common ground and reserve difference. It is evident that both "unity of Heaven and human" and Morrison attach great importance to family ethical relationships and emphasizes the necessity of building harmonious and healthy relationships with others. Both aim to call for the elimination of discrimination among different races, gender, and class and establish a harmonious social environment for everyone in the world.

The ultimate and highest goal of "unity of Heaven and human" is for an individual to achieve harmony with the inner self. Impacted by industrialization and the alienated relation with nature and society, human inner world had been dramatically distorted. They suffer from spiritual crisis because of the disharmonious relationship between body and mind, which, at the same time, hinders their construction of self-identity. Identity-construction has always been Morrison's concern in her works. Characters in her novels are absent of self-identity because of their loss of morality and virtues as well as their awareness of self-love and self-value. Industrialization makes human concern more about material and wealth accumulation with unlimited desire, which leads to human's deformed value system without morality and virtue. In *Sula, A Mercy, Paradise*, Morrison describes Sula, Jacob, and Morgan brothers' loss of self-identity because of the absence of morality and virtues. Because of the discrimination and inequality in society, human feels self-loathing and inferior to their existence, and suffers the spiritual crisis. The distorted human nature, the split within themselves, and the reverse value system are the manifestations of their spiritual crisis. With regards to the relationship with the inner self, "unity of Heaven and human" emphasizes that morality and virtues are the basic requirements for achieving harmony with the inner self. A person needs morality and virtues to guide his words and deeds to become an authentic human being. On the contrary, people without morality and virtues would misconduct his behaviors when interacting with others in society, which harm the benefits of others as well as his self-development.

Apart from morality and virtues, the awareness of self-love and self-value also contribute to human's construction of self-identity. It asks an individual to realize his value as a human being. In Morrison's novels, African Americans have been degraded and devalued by the whites because of their skin color, which leads to their sense of inferiority and self-denial. In order to construct their sense of self-identity, the first step for them is to love and value themselves from the inner world. The next step is to accept their racial identity and racial culture to regain their sense of rootedness in society. In *Paradise* and *God Help the Child*, Consolata and Bride are the typical characters who are bestowed with self-love and self-value and finally fulfill their construction of self-identity. Morrison depicts these characters who realize their spiritual freedom, and guide other people to construct sound self-identities. Both Morrison and Confucianism attach great importance to morality and virtues and the sense of self-love and self-value to human's self-identity construction.

In summary, both Confucian "unity of Heaven and human" and Morrison are concerned about the development and destiny of whole human beings, such as how to realize the sustainable development of human society, how to deal with the relationship between human and nature, between human and society, and relations with the inner self. To maintain a dynamic, harmonious, peaceful relationship between nature, human and self is not at all an easy thing, it is an ever-lasting practice for humankind. "Unity of Heaven and human" provides precious teachings and principles for humankind to direct their behaviors. Morrison also demonstrates her concern for the development of human beings with her outstanding works. This study is significant because it not only examines the connection between Confucianism and Morrison, but also addresses issues such as race, gender, family, as well as the relationship with nature and the inner self. It is a good try if we solve these problems with the philosophical wisdom embedded in Confucianism and Morrison's works. Both offer a solution to eliminate the current injustice and inequality in the world. That is love. Love can overcome the frustrations and relieve tensions among parents, children, women, men; love is the key element to solve the problems of nature, gender, and race; and love is the key element needed when we construct a harmonious society.

Bibliography

ALWES D, 1996. The burden of liberty: choice in Toni Morrison's *Jazz* and Toni Cade Barbara's *The Salt Eaters*[J]. African American review, 30 (3): 353-365.

AMES R T, ROSEMONT H Jr., 2010. The analects of Confucius: a philosophical translation[M]. New York: Random House Publishing Group.

ANDERSON M R, 2013. Spectrality in the novels of Toni Morrison[M]. Knoxville, TN: University of Tennessee Press.

ANNE-MARIE P D, 2001. Toni Morrison's *Jazz* and *The City*[J]. African American review, 35 (2): 219.

ANNPING C, 2014. The analects (Lun Yu) [M]. New York: Penguin Group (USA) LLC.

AOI M, 1999. Toni Morrison and womanish discourse [M]. New York: Peter Lang Publishing.

BEAULIEU E A, 1999. Black women writers and the American neo-slave narrative: femininity unfettered[M]. London: Praeger.

BEAVERS H, 1998. The politics of space: southernness and manhood in the fictions of Toni Morrison[J]. Studies in the literary imagination, 31 (2): 61-77.

BELL B W, 1992. *Beloved*: a womanist neo-slave narrative or multivocal remembrances of things past[J]. African American review, 26 (1): 7-15.

BIRCH E L, 1994. Black American writings: a quilt of many colors[M]. Coleshilll, Birmingham: Harvester Wheatsheaf.

BJORK P B, 1996. The novels of Toni Morrison: the search for self and place within the community[M]. New York: Peter Lang Inc.

BLOOM H, 1990. Toni Morrison[M]. New York: Chelsea House Publishers.

BLYDEN E W, 1967. Christianity, Islam, and the negro race [M]. Edinburgh: Edinburgh University Press.

BOUDREAU K, 2001. Pain and the unmaking of self in Toni Morrison's *Beloved* [J]. Contemporary literature, 36 (3): 447-465.

BROWN S A, 1966. A century of negro portraiture in American literature[J].The Massachusetts review, 7 (1): 73-96.

BRYANT C G, 1990. The orderliness of disorder: madness and evil in Toni Morrison's *Sula*[J]. Black American literature forum, 24 (4): 731-745.

BUSS D, DIDI H, 2003. Globalizing family values[M]. Minneapolis: University of Minnesota Press.

BYERMAN K E, 1990. Beyond realism: the fictions of Toni Morrison [M]// BLOOM S. Modern critical views: Toni Morrison. New York: Chelsea House.

CADY L V, 1961. Thoreau's quotations from the Confucian books in *Walden*[J]. American literature, 33 (1): 20-32.

CARBY H V, 1992. Reconstructing womanhood: the emergence of the Afro-American woman novelist[M]. Oxford: Oxford University Press.

CARUS T L, 2004. De rerum natura[M]. BAO L M, trans. Beijing: China Social Science Press.

CHENG H, CHENG Y, 1981. The anthology of Cheng Hao and Cheng Yi[M]. Beijing: Zhonghua Book Company.

CHRISTIAN B, 1980. Community and nature: the novels of Toni Morrison[J]. Journal of ethnic and cultural studies, 7 (4): 65-78.

CHRISTIAN B, 1985. Black feminist criticism: perspectives on black women writers[M]. New York: Pergamon.

COPELAND R S, 1971. Community origins of the black power movement[M]. New York: Crowell.

DAVIDSON R, 2001. Racial stock and 8-rocks: communal historiography in Toni Morrison's *Paradise*[J]. Nineteenth-century literature, 47 (3): 355-373.

DAVIS A Y, 2000. Women, race & class[M]. New York: Vintage Books.

DAVIS C B, 2002. Black women: writing and identity: migration of the subject [M]. London: Routledge.

DENARD C, 1988. The convergence of feminism and ethnicity in the fiction of Toni Morrison[M]//MCKAY. Critical essays on Toni Morrison. Boston: G. K. Hall.

DONG Z S, 2001. Deep perception for the name[M]//ZHOU G D, PENG X, trans. The various revelation of spring and autumn. Jinan: Shandong Friendship Press.

DONG Z S, 2011. Spring and autumn annals[M]. ZHOU G X, trans. Beijing: Zhonghua Book Company.

DONG Z S, 2015. Luxuriant gems of the spring and autumn annals[M]. SARAH Q, JOHN M, trans. New York: Columbia University Press.

DUAN J Z, 1995. On the relationship of family and society[J]. Journal of Shanxi university of finance and economics (6): 81-83.

DUBEY M, 1997. "No bottom and no top": oppositions in *Sula*[M]//PEACH L. Toni Morrison: contemporary critical essays. New York, NY: St. Martins's.

EINSTEIN A, 1996. The collected papers of Albert Einstein[M]. Princeton, NJ: Princeton University Press.

EYERMAN R, 2001. Cultural trauma: slavery and the formation of African American identity[M]. New York: Cambridge University Press.

FARSHID S, 2015. The crucial role of naming in Toni Morrison's *Song of Solomon*[J]. Journal of African American studies, 19: 329-338.

FITZGERALD J, 1993. Selfhood and community: psychoanalysis and discourse in *Beloved*[J]. Modern fiction studies, 39 (3/4): 669-687.

FLYS J C, 1993. Time as geography in *Song of Solomon*[M]. Reden: Revista Espanola De Estudios Norteamericanos.

FOWLER D, 2011. "Nobody could make it alone": fathers and boundaries in Toni Morrison's *Beloved*[J]. MELUS (multi-ethnic literature of the U.S.), 36 (2): 13-33.

FOX-GENOVESE E, 1998. The freedom of the human person: connection or disconnection[M]. New York: Institute for American Values.

FREIERT W, 1983. Classical themes in *Song of Solomon*[J]. Helos, 10: 161-170.

FROMM E, 2006. The art of loving[M]//ABBEY E. Harper Perennial modern classics. New York: Harper Perennial.

FRYE N, 2002. The great code: *The Bible* and literature[M]. Boston: Mariner Books.

FUQUA A, 2012. The furrow of his brow: providence and pragmatism in Toni Morrison's *Paradise*[J]. The midwest quarterly, 54 (1): 38-52.

FURMAN J, 1996. Community and cultural identity[M]//MIDDLETON D L. Toni Morrison's fiction. Columbia, SC: University of South Carolina Press.

GATES H L Jr., 1989. The signifying monkey: a theory of African-American literary criticism[M]. Oxford: Oxford University Press.

GATES H L Jr., APPIAH K A, 1993. Toni Morrison: critical perspective past and present[M]. New York: Amistad.

GIDDENS A, 1991. Modernity and self-identity[M]. Cambridge: Polity Press.

GILLESPIE C, 2007. Critical companion to Toni Morrison: a literary reference to her life and work[M]. New York: Infobase Publishing.

GRAHAM G, 1989. The morality of groups[J]. Analytic philosophy, 30: 240-242.

GREWAL G, 1998. Circles of sorrow, lines of struggle: the novels of Toni Morrison[M]. Baton Rouge: LSU Press.

HALPER J, 2012. Misery and company: Sigmund Freud's presence in Toni Morrison's *Beloved*[J]. Articulāte, 17 (6): 42-47.

HARDING W, JACKY M, 1994. A world of difference: an inter-cultural study of Toni Morrison's novels [M]. Westport: Greenwood Press.

HARRIS T, 1988. Reconnecting fragments: Afro-American folk tradition in *The Bluest Eye*[M]//MCKAY N Y. Critical essays on Toni Morrison. Boston: G. K. Hall & Co.

HARRIS T, 1991. Fiction and folklore: the novels of Toni Morrison [M]. Knoxville: The University of Tennessee Press.

HATHAWAY H, 2019. Rewriting race, gender and religion in Toni Morrison's *Song of Solomon* and *Paradise*[J]. Religions, 10 (6): 345.

HEINER J L J, 2008. Narrative conventions and race in the novels of Toni Morrison[M]. London: Routledge.

HIGGINS T E, 2001. Religiosity, cosmology, and folklore: the African influence in the novels of Toni Morrison[M]. London: Routledge.

HINSON D S, 2001. Narrative and community crisis in *Beloved*[J]. African American literature, 26 (4): 147-167.

HOLLYWAY K C, 1987. New dimensions of spiritually: a biracial and bicultural reading of the novels of Toni Morrison[M]. New York: Greenwood.

HONG Y, 2018. The sinitic civilization book II: a factual history through the lens of archaeology, bronzeware, calendar, and the annals[M]. Seoul: IUniverse.

HOOKS B,1990. Yearning: race, gender, and cultural politics [M]. Boston: South End.

HOOKS B, 2002. "Touching the earth" city wilds: essays and stories about urban nature[M]. Athens: University of Georgia Press.

HSUN T, 2009. Full translation of the works of Hsun Tzu[M]. Guiyang: Guizhou People's Press.

HU J, 2007. African-Americans' quest for identity: a study of Toni Morrison's novels[M]. Beijing: Beijing Press.

HUNT K, 2000. Paradise lost: the destructive forces of double consciousness and boundaries in Toni Morrison's paradise [C]//TALLMADGE J, HARRINGTON H. Reading under the sign of nature: new essays in ecocriticism. Salt Lake: University of Utah Press.

IMBRIE A E, 1993. "What Shalimar knew": Toni Morrison's *Song of Solomon* as a pastoral novel[J]. College English, 55 (5): 473-490.

JI X L, 2011. Ji Xianlin on culture[M]. 1st ed. Beijing: People's Daily Press.

JIAO X T, 2006. Pluralistic dreams: the aesthetic of the quilt and Toni Morrison's political appeal[D]. Zhengzhou: Henan University.

JIAO X T, 2016. Literary sentiment: interview with Toni Morrison[J]. Foreign language and literature, 32 (4): 1-4.

JONES B W, ANDREY L V, 1985. The world of Toni Morrison: explorations in literary criticism[M]. Dubuque, IA: Kendall Hunt Pub Co.

KANT I, 1999. Critique of judgment[M]. Beijing: China Social Sciences Press.

KAPLAN C, NORMA A, MINO M, 1999. Between women and nation: nationalisms, transnational feminisms, and the state[M]. Durham, NC: Duke University Press.

KATHIR T I, 1938. The meaning of the glorious Quran[M]. Hyderabad-Deccan: Government Central Press.

KING J, 2000. Women and the word[M]. London: Palgrave Macmillan.

KOENER A, 1984. The one out of sequence: an interview with Toni Morrison[J]. History and tradition in Afro-American culture, 16 (1/2): 273-283.

KRUMHOLZ L, 1992. The ghosts of slavery: historical recovery in Toni Morrison's *Beloved*[J]. African American review, 26 (3): 395-408.

KUENZ J, 1994. *The Bluest Eye*: notes on history, community, and black females subjectivity[J]. African American review, 27 (3): 421-431.

LAO T, 1999. Tao De Ching[M]//CHEN C J. All classes of philosophers. Xining: Qinghai People's Press.

LEE C C, 1998. The south in Toni Morrison's *Song of Solomon*: initiation, healing and home[J]. Studies in the literary imagination, 31 (2): 109-123.

LEE D H, 1982. *Song of Solomon*: to ride the air[J]. Black American literature forum, 16: 64-70.

LEOPOLD A, 1986. A sand county almanac[M]. 7th ed. New York: Ballantine Books.

LILFRICH C, 2006. Anti-exodus: countermemory, gender, race and everyday life in Toni Morrison's *Paradise* [J]. Modern fiction studies, 52 (2): 321-349.

LU S Y, 2000. Ecological and art literature [M]. Xi'an: Shaanxi People Education Press.

LV B W, 2010. The spring and autumn of Lv［M］. WANG X M, anno. Nanchang: Jiangxi People's Press.

MARSHALL P, 1984. The chosen place, the timeless people［M］. London: Vintage.

MASON T O Jr., 1988. The novelist as conservator: stories and comprehension in Toni Morrison's *Song of Solomon*［J］. Contemporary literature, 29 (4): 564-581.

MBALIA D D, 1991. Toni Morrison's developing class consciousness［M］. London: Associated University Press.

MBALIA D D, 1998. *Tar Baby*: a reflection of Morrison's developed class consciousness［M］//PEACH L. Toni Morrison. New York: St. Martin's.

MBITI J S, 1999. African religions, and philosophy［M］. 2nd ed. Oxford: Heinemann Education Publisher.

MCKAY N Y, 1983. An interview with Toni Morrison［J］. Contemporary literature, 24 (4): 413-429.

MCKAY N Y, 1988. Critical essays on Toni Morrison［M］. Boston: GK. Hall & Co.

MENG P Y, 1998. The Chinese philosophy of the unity of heaven and human and sustainable development［J］. History of Chinese philosophy (3): 35-37.

MENG P Y, 2007. The ecological significance and value of the study of humanity ［J］. History of Chinese philosophy (7): 10-15.

MILES M, SHIVA V, 1993. Ecofeminism［M］. London: Zed Books.

MORGENSTERN N, 2014. Maternal love/maternal violence: inventing ethics in Toni Morrison's *A Mercy*［J］. MELUS (Multi-ethnic literature of the U.S.), 39 (1): 7-29.

MORRIS S M, 2013. A past not pure but stifled: vexed legacies of leadership in Toni Morrison's *Love*［J］. South Atlantic quarterly, 112 (2): 319-338.

MORRISON T, 1970. The bluest eye［M］. New York: Washington Square Press.

MORRISON T, 1973. Sula［M］. New York: Alfred A. Knopf, Random House, Inc.

MORRISON T, 1977. Song of solomon［M］. New York: Alfred A. Knopf,

Random House, Inc.

MORRISON T, 1981. Tar baby[M]. New York: Alfred A. Knopf, Random House, Inc.

MORRISON T, 1992. Playing in the dark: whiteness and the literary imagination [M]. Cambridge: Harvard University Press.

MORRISON T, 1993. Jazz[M]. New York: Penguin Group.

MORRISON T, 1998. Paradise[M]. New York: Alfred A. Knopf, Random House, Inc.

MORRISON T, 2000. Beloved [M]. Beijing: Foreign Language Teaching and Research Press.

MORRISON T, 2003. Love[M]. London: Chatto & Windus.

MORRISON T, 2008. A mercy[M]. New York: Alfred A. Knopf, Random House, Inc.

MORRISON T, 2013. Home [M]. New York: Alfred A. Knopf, Random House, Inc.

MORRISON T, 2015. God helps the child [M]. New York: Alfred A. Knopf, Random House, Inc.

MUIR J, 1981. Our national parks[M]. Wisconsin: John University of Wisconsin Press.

MURPHY J M, 1988. Santeria: on African religion in America [M]. Boston: Beacon.

NI P M, 2016. Confucius: the man and the way of Gongfuzi[M]. Washington DC: Rowman & Littlefield Publishers.

NIE Z Z, 2011. Ethical literary criticism: ethical choice and Sphinx factor [J]. Foreign literature studies, 33 (6): 6-8.

O'REILLY A, 2004. Toni Morrison and motherhood: a politics of the heart [M]. Albany: State University of New York Press.

PAGE P, 1999. Reclaiming community in contemporary African-American fiction [M]. Oxford, MT: University Press of Mississippi.

PEACH L, 1998. Toni Morrison［M］. New York: St. Martin's Press.

QIAO Q J, 2011. On the ecological significance of benevolence［J］. History of Chinese philosophy (6): 19-21.

QIAO Q J, 2013. A survey of Confucian ecological thought［M］. Beijing: Peking University Press.

RAHMANI A, 2015. Black feminism: what women of color went through in Toni Morrison's selected novels ［J］. International journal of applied linguistics & English literature, 4 (3): 61.

REED H, 1988. Toni Morrison, *Song of Solomon* and black cultural nationalism ［J］. The centennial review, 32: 52.

RIGNEY B H, 1991. The voice of Toni Morrison［M］. Columbus: Ohio State University Press.

ROBERT S, 1994. Intimate things in place: a conversation with Toni Morrison ［M］//TAYLOR-GUTHRIE D. Conversations with Toni Morrison. Jackson: University Press of Mississippi.

ROMERO C, 2005. Creating the beloved community: religion, race, and nation in Toni Morrison's *Paradise*［J］. African American review, 39 (3): 415-430.

ROUSSEAU J-J, 2010. The social contract ［M］. Beijing: World Book Press.

RUAS C, 1985. Toni Morrison［M］//TAYLOR-GUTHRIE D. Conversation with Toni Morrison. Jackson: University Press of Mississippi.

RUETENIK T, 2010. Animal liberation or human redemption: racism and speciesism in Toni Morrison's *Beloved* ［J］. Interdisciplinary studies in literature and environment, 17 (2): 317-326.

SAMUELS W D, HUDSON-WEEMS C, 1990. Toni Morrison［M］. Boston: Twayne.

SCHREIBER E J, 2009. Race, trauma, and home in the novels of Toni Morrison ［M］. Baton Rouge, LA: LSU Press.

SHILAJA C L, 2015. Trauma and collective memory in Toni Morrison's *Beloved* and *A Mercy* ［J］. The IUP journal of English studies, X (4): 30-36.

SIMPSON R, 2007. Black looks & black acts［M］. New York: Peter Lang Inc.

SMITH B, 1978. Toward a black feminist criticism [M]//The center for critical education. The radical teacher. Fitchburg, WI: University of Illinois Press.

SMITH E R, MACKIE D M, 2007. Social psychology [M]. 3rd ed. Hove: Psychology Press.

SMITH V, 1985. The quest for and discovery of identity in Toni Morrison's *Song of Solomon*[J]. Southern review, 21 (3): 721.

SNIADER L S, 1992. Fictions of authority: women writers and narrative voice [M]. Ithaca, NY: Cornell University Press.

SPOTTKE N, 2009. Coffins, closets, kitchens, and convents: women writing of home in gendered space[D]. Tampa, FL: University of South Florida.

STEPTO R, 1991. Conversations with Toni Morrison[M]. New York: Library of Congress.

SUSAN L B, 1980. Folklore and community in *Song of Solomon*[M]. Oxford: Oxford University Press.

TAMILSELVI, A, PRABHA R W, 2016. Discovery of "self" and "identity" of Afro-Americans in Toni Morrison's *Sula* and *Tar Baby*[J]. International journal on studies in English language and literature, 4: 79-84.

TATE C, 1984. Black women writers at work[M]. 1st ed. London: Continuum Intl Pub Group.

TAYLOR-GUTHRIE D, 1994. Conversation with Toni Morrison [M]. Jackson: University Press of Mississippi.

TU W M, 1998. Epilogue: human rights as a Confucian moral discourse[M]. New York: Columbia University Press.

VALERIE S, 2003. The quest for and discovery of identity in Toni Morrison's *Song of Solomon*[M]//FURMAN J. Toni Morrison's *Song of Solomon*: a casebook. New York: Oxford University Press.

VARSAVA J A, 2002. Review: the dialectics of self and community in Toni Morrison and Thomas Pynchon[J]. Contemporary literature, 43 (4): 794-803.

VISSER I, 2014. Entanglements of trauma: relationality and Toni Morrison's *Home*

［J］. Postcolonial text, 9 (2): 1-21.

WAIGUCHU J M, 1971. Black heritage of genetics, environment, and continuity ［M］//GOLDSTEIN R L. Black life and culture in the United States. New York: Apollo Editions.

WANG G X, LI X M, 2009. The family analects of Confucius［M］. Beijing: Zhonghua Book Company.

WANG S R, WU X Y, 1997. Gender, race, culture: Toni Morrison and 20th century African-American literature［M］. Beijing: Peking University Press.

WANG S R, WU X Y, 2004. A new thought on love: a review of Morrison's *Love* ［J］. Contemporary foreign literature, 2: 43-53.

WANG Y K, 2005. A study of Toni Morrison ［M］. Beijing: People's Literature Publishing House.

WANG Z R, WEN R Y, 2013. A collection of doctrine of the mean［M］. Beijing: The Chinese Overseas Publishing House.

WARREN K J, 1996. Ecological feminist philosophy ［M］. Bloomington: Indiana University Press.

WEEVER D J, 1979. The inverted world of Toni Morrison's *The Bluest Eye* and *Sula*［J］. CLA journal, 16 (1): 402-413.

WEGS J M, 1982. Toni Morrison's *Song of Solomon*: a blues song［J］. Essays in literature, 9: 211.

WHITE J F, 2013. Two Vashtis: Morrison's *Beloved* and *The Book of Esther*［J］. Taylor & Francis online, 71 (3): 188-190.

WIJEYESINGHE C L, BAILEY W J III, 2001. New perspectives on racial identity development: a theoretical and practical anthology ［M］. New York: New York University Press.

WOLFF C, 1991. Margaret Garner: a Cincinnati story［J］. Massachusetts review, 32 (2): 60.

ZHANG B Q, 2007. Analects ［M］. Guilin: Lijiang Press.

ZHANG D N, 1982. Outline of Chinese philosophy［M］. 1st ed. Beijing: Chinese

Social Sciences Press.

ZHANG R W, 2006. A study of Toni Morrison [M]. Beijing: Foreign Language Teaching and Research Press.

ZHANG Z, 2009. Words by master Zhang [M]. WANG F Z, trans. Beijing: Zhonghua Book Company.

ZHAO L H, 2011. Space politics: a study of Toni Morrison's novels [M]. Chengdu: Sichuan University Press.

ZHEN D, 1982. The meaning card of the works of Mencius[M]. 1st ed. Beijing: Zhonghua Book Company.

ZHEN D, 2009. Original compassion[M]. 1st ed. Shanghai: Ancient Books Press.

ZHU X, 1986, Classified dialogues of master Zhu[M]. Beijing: Zhonghua Book Company.

ZHU X L, 2008. Violent world in Toni Morrison's novels [J]. Foreign literature review, 2: 168-176.

Acknowledgement

Recalling the long journey to write the book, I find there are so many people that I should extend my thanks to for this book would not have been possible without their patience, encouragement and support.

First and foremost, I owe the greatest debt to Prof. Choi Hie Sup, my doctoral supervisor. Without his enlightenment and supervision during the last two years, the completion of this book would be impossible. Thanks for his keen observations and indispensable guidance during the whole process from the conception to composition of this book. Thanks for all of his concerns and priceless suggestions that make me capable of understanding research related work and idea generation at the time of writing my book. I admire Prof. Choi's affability, his sense of humor and his persistence in pursuing his beloved research field. He is the best professor as well as the person I have ever met.

I can never adequately thank Prof. Shin Dong Jin for his constant support, advice, and encouragement which make my study and life at Jeonju University interesting and unforgettable. He is so generous and supportive during the period of my study in Korea. He always inspires and helps me a lot to make my Korean life comfortable. His advice and insight have stimulated my imagination and pushed me to see beyond my complacencies.

I offer my gratitude also to Prof. Cho Eun Young who has read my first and last draft word by word and made many valuable corrections and inspiring criticisms by which the present version has been noticeably improved. I am also profoundly grateful to Prof. Hwang Yo Han and Prof. Choi Joong Yeol for being so cooperative and letting my defense be a pleasant moment, as well as for their valuable comments and suggestions. Their exemplary scholarship and dedication to their own studies have inspired me much in my book. The academic vision and personal gentleness of these professors set a good model for me in my work and life.

Thanks are also due to my fellow graduates students for their generous help, their moral support, or their valuable conversations about our studies, research, life, etc. My gratitude also goes to my friends in Korea for their moral support and assistance. Furthermore, I want to thank my friend David Shinay in America for his efforts to help me with the revision of my book.

Finally, I would like to express my deepest appreciation to my parents, to whom I dedicate my research work. They always show me the right path in every stage of my life. They have endured my complaints, and shared my sweet and bitter moments. Most important of all, loves me unconditionally as always. A special thanks to my beloved sister for her unconditional love, sacrifices, and encouragement that make me capable of coping with the unfavorable situations as well as challenges. Without her support, it was not possible to complete my study.